GOD'S
PRESCRIPTION

GOD'S
PRESCRIPTION

A Faith-Based Plan to Shift Your Mindset and Reclaim Your Natural Health

---

BY
TERRI WARD, MS, FNTP, CGP

Medical Disclaimer

Dedication

For those who long to honor their temples but have been led astray by a broken world—may you find wisdom, clarity, and the strength to reclaim your God-given health and fulfill your purpose with energy and vitality.

Praises for
God's Prescription...

"At a time when the 'sickcare' model profits from symptom suppression, *God's Prescription* is a bold call to return to God's original design for healing. Terri Ward doesn't just point out what's broken—she offers truth, wisdom, and a faith-based framework to help readers rise above a system that too often leaves them sick, confused, and disempowered. This book is a gift to the body of Christ and to anyone who longs to feel vibrant, connected, and strong in their body, mind, and spirit. *God's Prescription* is a powerful resource for anyone committed to root-cause healing and whole-person transformation."

—Dr. Michael Karlfeldt, ND, PhD,
Founder of The Karlfeldt Center;
Author of *A Better Way to Treat Cancer*

"*God's Prescription* is a thoughtful guide that seamlessly blends personal anecdotes, historical context, and actionable health insights for anyone seeking to reclaim their well-being. Terri Ward's engaging writing style demystifies complex topics, making understanding and applying practical lifestyle shifts easier. While the book is rooted in a faith-based perspective, it remains accessible for readers from all backgrounds by focusing on tangible, long-term health strategies. It's a fresh, relatable resource that empowers you to take charge of your vitality without feeling overwhelmed."

—Dr. George Birnbach

"When I first read an article by Terri Ward in *The Epoch Times*, I was impressed. 'Who is this?' I wondered. 'She isn't some crackpot spouting off theories or textbook drivel. Nor is she an industry shill, parroting the propaganda I see every day on the networks and in mainstream medical news posts. She actually knows her stuff. And it's based on solid science!' I thought nothing more of it after sharing my thoughts in the Comments section…until my chiropractor told me her mother appreciated my endorsement of her article. 'What? Terri is your mother? Small world!'

Seeing the depth of Terri's knowledge and the quality of her research, I was more than happy to accept the invitation to review *God's Prescription*. As a Christian, healer, and specialist in Functional, Metabolic, and Regenerative Medicine, I cannot endorse this book highly enough. Page after page, I kept saying to myself, 'Yes, yes, YES!' Terri's assessment of the state of medical care in America is spot on, and her orderly delivery of *God's prescription* for healing is exactly what each of us needs.

There is no theory or opinion here. Everything espoused in these pages is Biblical, confirmed by scientific studies, and practical. This book is so factual, easy to read, comprehensive, and helpful that I insist on having copies in my offices and encourage my patients to read and apply it. Additionally, I've given copies to each of my children to help them get my grandchildren started off on the right foot in life.

The more people follow *God's Prescription*, the fewer will need to see doctors such as myself for cancer, autoimmune diseases, chronic pain, diabetes, autism, mental and behavioral disorders, and the other complex conditions which have become epidemic in modern American society. This is because, even though Terri Ward put the words on each page of this book, the real author is the Master Healer."

—Ray Andrew, MD

"Terri Ward's new book *God's Prescription* is not just another manual for physical health; it is a spiritual journey on a holistic path to wellness that encourages readers to reclaim their well-being through the wisdom of biblical Scripture and current scientific insights. This integration of science and spirituality empowers individuals with clarity and courage to break free from the confusions and restrictive mindset often associated with mainstream health practices.

The book is filled with practical advice on how to use God's Word to reclaim health. Readers will find practical advice, heartfelt stories, and actionable strategies designed to inspire and motivate. Terri's passion for helping others is evident in her writing, as she encourages readers to embrace the God-given health and discover the joy of living a vibrant life. With a focus on clean, organic ingredients and allergy-friendly options through her company, Spice Cure, Terri aims to make healthy eating enjoyable and sustainable.

As a functional nutritionist with a Master of Science in Human Nutrition and Functional Medicine, Terri draws from her personal experiences and professional expertise to guide individuals facing health challenges. After years of struggling with her own health issues as a former Certified Public Accountant, she understands the emotional and physical toll that poor health can take. Her story of overcoming pain and inflammation through nutrition and lifestyle changes serves as a beacon of hope for those who feel lost in their health journey.

Her previous works, including *Alkaline Diet Meal Prep* and *The Healing Diverticulitis Cookbook*, showcase her commitment to creating accessible health resources that empower individuals to make informed choices about their nutrition. Terri Ward's heartfelt insights and practical advice make this book a valuable resource for anyone seeking to honour their body and spirit in a changing world."

—Rahat Iram, MD

"We are wonderfully and fearfully made by God, which means we are complex beings. In *God's Prescription*, Terri does a wonderful job of connecting the dots together from God's word, our current culture, and how He designed our bodies to work. She presents a great balance of information and practical steps towards a healthier life."

—Pastor Brian Seidel,
Faith Journey Church,
Caldwell, ID

"I know Terri personally, and I can honestly say this incredible, awesome book has been written under the inspiration of the Holy Spirit. I don't say that to take away from all that she has studied and poured herself into—only that from beginning to end you can witness the divine inspiration.

Proverbs 4:7 says, 'Wisdom is the principal thing; therefore get wisdom. And in all your getting, get understanding.'

That's what Terri has laid before us in her book—saturated with love and care for others to have a healthy lifestyle.

Or as 3 John 2 puts it: 'Beloved, I pray that you may prosper in all things and be in health, just as your soul prospers.'

Well done, Terri. I'm looking forward to my own copies!"

—Rev. Leslie A. Green,
Associate Pastor, Messiah Ministries Church Inc.,
Oklahoma City, OK

"As a retired Army chaplain, and now as a professor and mental health professional, I am pleased to give my full endorsement for this incredible book. The author masterfully writes from the foundational truth of God's Word, sharing insight and practical wisdom that will help us care for our body, the temple of the Holy Spirit. This book can help you live an abundant and healthy life."

—Mark Knox, Ph.D., D.Min., LMFT,
Army Chaplain (Retired),
Counseling Professor

"I have known Terri for over 40 years. She is a smart, motivated lifelong student with a strong moral compass. If you want to take an active role in your health and be part of the solution instead of part of the problem, you will benefit from her years of knowledge and experience. She has done the research and the work, so you, the reader, don't have to."

—Dr. Don Hecht

"An enlightening read that beautifully explores the powerful connection between comprehensive health, oral health, and over wellness. This book offers practical insights into how natural healing can transform your dental health and beyond, empowering readers to take control of their well-being in a holistic way. A must-read for anyone seeking a healthier, more natural approach to oral and overall health care."

—Luke Jacobsen, DDS

"So much has changed in our world. *God's Prescription* is a book for our time. It is full of thought provoking and practical insights to illuminate our complicated journey toward health and healing."

—Patricia, Cook, LFMT

"Finally, a connection between the Maker of the body and our health. Terri has done an excellent job of providing scriptural principles for health actions. I plan to suggest it to all my patients who are seeking ways to improve their health. I haven't seen anything like it—lots of books on functional medicine principles, but this book gives clear, concise guidelines for consideration and it is based on the Bible. Who better to give new life to our bodies than the One who gives new life? A must for every thoughtful Christian who values their health. Also, a must for those who are wondering why their body has gone awry but have no idea that God might have thoughts about their health."

—Wallene A Stoddard, CNM, MS

"Terri Ward has written an easy-to-read book that elegantly combines God's Word with scientific research. She clearly shows how God's original design for health and wellness is still relevant today, using Scriptures as the foundation and science to support it. This book is a powerful reminder that healing begins with God's Word. Clinicians should be prescribing *God's Prescription* to patients seeking true restoration – body, mind, and spirit."

—Sergey Kashubin, NP-C

"*God's Prescription* by Terri Ward is insightful, provocative, and possibly the wisdom that could save your life. It not only exposes our destructive processed food and healthcare system, but it reveals a roadmap for what you can do to find real health, reduce sickness and disease, and discover the total health that we all desperately desire."

—Bill Dolan, Spirit Media

"*God's Prescription* is an amazing book that is packed with valuable information. It is easy to read and incredibly educational, backed by eye-opening facts and biblical truths. This book is a must-read for anyone who wants to take charge of their health and live the abundant life that Jesus has promised us."

—Galina Kashubin

Contents

Foreword

by Mario Murillo

Who can you trust? That is the big question when it comes to health. We are bombarded by lies and scams. You will hear promises of great results. They will tell you wild theories of what is wrong with your body. Then there is the mixture of Eastern Religion in health regimens. The health landscape is riddled with quacks after a fast buck.

Even in the church there has been a great deal of bad advice and bad habits. For example: it makes no sense to claim all of God's promises of healing while you violate all of God's laws for health. But there is an answer we can trust.

Finally, here is a book that breaks it down. You can trust it because it is grounded in both good science and—most importantly—in the Word of God.

God's Prescription by Terri Ward is your answer to a real, practical change in your health. What you get is a road map that makes sense. You will see the root of our health crisis in America. Then you will learn all the vital connections God created that make your body work.

This is the perfect time for this book. America, under the leadership of Robert F. Kennedy Jr., is in a health revolution. The church should be ahead of the curve. We have the edge through our Lord Jesus Christ.

Psalm 103, verse 5 (MEV) says, "Who satisfies your mouth with good things, so that your youth is renewed like the eagle's."

—Mario Murillo, Evangelist and Best-Selling Author

Foreword

by Dr. John Bartemus

This new book by Terri is timely given the current state of human health. And if it has the impact that I believe God wants it to have, *God's Prescription* will also be timeless.

The origin story and the solution to the debacle known as mainstream medicine is beautifully laid out within these pages. As was made abundantly clear by the COVID-19 pandemic, the current model of what is inaccurately called "healthcare" in the Western world does anything but create health.

In fact, it does the opposite. Therefore, we should refer to it by a name that describes what is accomplished by its machinations…Sickcare.

Chapter 2 reveals that the current sickcare model was created not to promote health or healing, but to create and monopolize a new industry: the "healthcare" industry. Today, modern medicine is owned by corporations. What is the goal of a corporation?

To make its shareholders money.

In fact, it is against the interests of any corporation to operate in a way that will lose the shareholders money. If you are healthy and avoid being trapped on the sickcare hamster wheel will the corporations make money? No.

This is why the sickcare model is built on treating symptoms and not on finding and addressing the cause(s) of a person's illness. If you find and address the cause(s) then the person is healed and no longer in the system. The system loses a patient and the associated money. Shareholders are unhappy.

On the other hand, symptom suppression never ends; it creates a patient for life. If you stop suppressing symptoms then the symptoms come back. Therefore, your doctor tells you that you must stay on your drug for the rest of your life. Tell that to millions of people every day and you have quite a lucrative business model.

Need proof? According to an article published on Fortune.com in September 2024, Novo Nordisk, the pharmaceutical company that owns Ozempic (Semaglutide), is now worth more than the entire gross domestic product (GDP) of the nation in which it resides (Denmark).[1]

Ozempic doesn't address the cause. Ozempic doesn't make you healthy. Even when it accomplishes its stated goal of helping you lose weight Ozempic makes you less healthy and closer to death via suicidal ideation in up to 45% of patients,[2] a 9× increased risk of pancreatitis, a 4× greater risk of bowel obstruction, and an over 3.5× increased risk of gastroparesis.[3] You will learn in chapter 6 how damaging the gastrointestinal (GI) tract damages the entire body.

God's prescription is not Ozempic or any other man-made drug. God's prescription is to address the cause(s) so that you can fulfill His purposes for you on this planet.

"Do you not know that you are God's temple and that God's Spirit dwells in you? If anyone destroys God's temple, God will destroy him. For God's temple is holy, and you are that temple." (1 Cor. 3:16-17, ESV).

God's Prescription was written to help you recognize that following the sickcare model of health is destroying your temple. *God's Prescription* is a blueprint for stopping the destruction of your temple no matter how much damage you have sustained to this point. *God's Prescription* is a blueprint for remodeling your temple and restoring it to the palace that God intended.

God's Prescription is for us to be good stewards of the Earthly vessel He has gifted each of us.

"Do you not know that your bodies are temples of the Holy Spirit, who is in you, whom you have received from God? You are not your own; you were bought at a price. Therefore honor God with your body." (1 Cor 6:19-20, *NIV*).

We cannot honor God and achieve all that He intends for us if we make choices that make us unhealthy. We cannot make healthy choices if we do not educate ourselves on how to create and sustain optimal health.

"My people are destroyed for a lack of knowledge." (Hos 4:6, *ESV*).

I believe the Holy Spirit breathed His prescription, *God's Prescription*, into the heart, mind, and soul of Terri Ward in order to provide His people with the roadmap to Godly health.

Let us all take notice of God's instruction, and the teaching and role-modeling of practitioners of true, Godly healthcare like Terri. And more than take notice, let us take action!

"For the kingdom of God does not consist in talk but in power." (1 Cor 4:20, *ESV*).

"Do you not know that in a race all the runners run, but only one receives the prize? So run that you may obtain it...I do not run aimlessly; I do not box as one beating the air. But I discipline my body and keep it under control, lest after preaching to others I myself should be disqualified." (1 Cor 9:24, 26-27, *ESV*).

—Dr. John Bartemus, DC, BCIM, CFMP
International best-selling author of *The Autoimmune Answer*

References:

1. Sjolin, Sara, et al. "Novo Nordisk's Market Value of $570 Billion Is More than Denmark's Annual GDP." *Fortune Europe*, Fortune, 23 Sept. 2024, fortune.com/europe/2024/09/23/novo-nordisk-nokia-risk-mette-frederiksen-denmark/.

2. Schoretsanitis G, Weiler S, Barbui C, Raschi E, Gastaldon C. Disproportionality Analysis From World Health Organization Data on Semaglutide, Liraglutide, and Suicidality. *JAMA Netw Open.* 2024;7(8):e2423385. doi:10.1001/jamanetworkopen.2024.23385

3. Sodhi M, Rezaeianzadeh R, Kezouh A, Etminan M. Risk of Gastrointestinal Adverse Events Associated With Glucagon-Like Peptide-1 Receptor Agonists for Weight Loss. *JAMA.* 2023;330(18):1795–1797. doi:10.1001/jama.2023.19574

Introduction

Are you a Christian who wants to honor God with your health, but you...

- Struggle with your weight or health issues?
- Feel too busy to work out or prepare meals?
- Are confused by conflicting health advice?
- Think you've already tried it all?

I get it. Staying healthy in a fallen world isn't easy. Even churches don't help when they serve cookies and donuts every week!

- 60% of American adults have a chronic lifestyle disease.
- 74% are overweight.
- 40% are expected to get cancer.

When Jesus walked the earth, He wasn't surrounded by engineered food products and environmental toxins, nor did He have a sedentary lifestyle. Today, it's a minefield of vulnerability!

If any of this resonates, *God's Prescription* was written for you. Whether you're claiming the health that's rightfully yours or reclaiming it, this book will help you connect the dots between Scripture, science, and soundness of body, mind, and spirit. It will clarify the steps to reclaim and sustain your health long-term.

Before we begin, I want to introduce myself and share more of what this book is—and isn't—about.

I'm Terri Ward, a recovering Certified Public Accountant (CPA). After many *taxing* years as a CPA, my health was suffering and my passion was fading. My gut was a mess! My pain and inflammation were out of control. I remember standing in the kitchen crying. My husband asked what was wrong, and I said, "I'm afraid I'm going to feel like this forever, and you won't understand and will be frustrated with me."

Thankfully, I was able to heal my gut and restore my health through nutrition and lifestyle changes. Then came my *ah-ha* moment. I realized the health issues that caused me to change my diet were a blessing, not a curse. They ultimately made me healthier, and I felt a deep calling to help others do the same. So, I went back to school, earned a Master of Science degree in Human Nutrition and Functional Medicine, plus two nutrition certifications.

As a functional nutritionist, I help people heal their guts and take back their health with sustainable, actionable game plans. Most of my clients don't know what to eat when they first see me. I help them eliminate the confusion and cut years off the struggle of figuring it out alone.

One day, God told me to tell His people that our food and healthcare systems are *not* what He intended. I wish I could say I jumped into action, but I procrastinated for years, afraid of alienating non-believers. Finally, I took a leap of faith, started writing, and stopped hiding my light under a bushel.

My goal with this book is to help you use God's Word to reclaim your health, so you can be and do all He intended. Armed with biblical wisdom and current science, communicated in a clear, practical way, you'll be empowered to make informed decisions.

The odds of death for our earthly life are still 100%. We can't change that, but we *can* change how we live and how we age. We each get one life, one body, and one brain—what we do with them is up to us. You have a purpose, but without health, how will you fulfill it?

*For we are God's handiwork, created in Christ Jesus to do good
works, which God prepared in advance for us to do.*

(Ephesians 2:10 *NIV*)

Have you ever experienced a sermon that made you squirm in your
seat? Some of the truths in these pages may challenge your personal
paradigm—perhaps even make you angry. I hope to awaken the lion
within you—to channel your frustrations into action, follow where
Scripture and science lead, and help you connect the dots.

God's Prescription is about truth and freedom! It's about reclaiming true
health and understanding *how* to honor your temple. It's about breaking free from the traps of our fallen world and strengthening your faith
along the way. Your health—and the health of future generations—
depends on it.

When I shared my vision with a pastor friend and mentioned enlisting
the church's support, he warned me it would be an uphill battle. He
was right. This *is* a battle—a spiritual battle—and it is my hope that
this book will open your eyes to that truth and so much more.

You will know the truth, and the truth will set you free.

(John 8:32 *CSB*)

You might think, "There's nothing new under the sun when it comes
to health advice." Eat less, move more... But what if much of what
you've been told is wrong? Conflicting health information is everywhere. 72% of U.S. adults say they regularly come across contradictory
nutrition information, making it harder to know what to trust.

God's Prescription cuts through the confusion, providing the tools and
a flexible framework to make sustainable, faith-based choices that
honor your body as a temple of the Holy Spirit. This isn't a quick fix,
but if you follow the steps in *God's Prescription*, you'll see positive results in just weeks.

Each chapter includes simple action steps to help you implement what you learn. References and resources for each chapter are available at https://terriward.com/gods-prescription-references/, where they can be regularly updated with the latest information.

In these pages, you'll learn:

- Why modern healthcare and food systems are failing us and how to take back control of your well-being.
- The deep connections between mind, body, and spirit, including your gut, brain, heart, mouth, and bone health—revealing how every part of your body is designed to work in harmony.
- How to build a sustainable, healthy lifestyle that nourishes your body and minimizes toxic burden.
- Practical tips on parenting and aging to equip the next generation for better health and help you navigate life's stages with grace and vitality.

Please remember, I'm just the messenger. Not everyone will agree with me, and that's okay. I'm still going to say it—because I care. Every position comes with a price, and every truth faces opposition—even God's truth.

This isn't another 40-day diet or fast. While *God's Prescription* clarifies what to eat and what to avoid, it's not a temporary diet—because temporary diets lead to temporary results. Instead, it's a lifestyle shift designed to extend your health span, giving you the energy and vitality to do what God has called you to do.

Will you take the GPS route programmed by a broken system that leads to dis-ease and medications and blame genetics, aging, or bad luck?

Or will you take the road less traveled – the path to true health and freedom outlined in *God's Prescription*?

Your health is your most valuable asset. You can spend years building wealth and dream of a life filled with travel, adventure, and leisure, but if you neglect your health and your body or brain fail you, it could all be for nothing.

I pray you'll join me on this journey. I pray the Holy Spirit makes this message relevant to you and finds your heart open.

> *I can do all things through Christ, who strengthens me.*
>
> (Philippians 4:13 *NKJV*)

Before we begin, a quick note—this book is not a substitute for medical advice. We will all face health challenges, but God has the power to overcome them.

When we align our lives with His design, we find the greatest joy, peace, and vitality.

Let's begin.

PART ONE

What Went Wrong?

The Constant in a Changing World

*The grass withers, the flower fades, But the
word of our God stands forever.*

(Isaiah 40:8 *NKJV*)

Aformer boss once told me the only thing constant is change. While change is indeed pervasive in our world, I know that God's nature and truth remain constant. As I finalize the manuscript for this book, potential big changes are on the horizon. On February 13, 2025, Robert F. Kennedy, Jr. was appointed Secretary of Health and Human Services (HHS) with a mission to Make America Healthy Again (MAHA).

President Trump has tasked Kennedy with significantly reducing childhood chronic disease within two years—a tall order. Kennedy is well-researched and understands the intricacies of government and politics intimately. His experience in environmental litigation and advocacy for children's health issues may serve him well in addressing this task.

His proposed agenda includes:

- Banning fluoride in drinking water.
- Ending FDA suppression of natural products like peptides and stem cells.
- Overhauling dietary guidelines.
- Reforming federal programs that subsidize ultra-processed foods.
- Reforming crop subsidies.
- Restricting harmful pesticides and chemicals.
- Restoring integrity to scientific research.
- Eliminating industries' capture and infiltration of governmental agencies.
- Restructuring patent royalties paid to government scientists.
- Requiring scientific safety testing for vaccines.
- Eliminating vaccine mandates.
- Ending direct-to-consumer advertising for prescription drugs.
- Redirecting research funding to preventive, alternative, and holistic therapies.
- Making infant formula safe, nutritious, and consistently available.

These are admirable goals, and as a nation, we desperately need to reclaim our health. Those who support this agenda look forward to its implementation, yet Kennedy faces significant opposition from entrenched interests across various sectors. Improving public health is complex, and opinions on these changes vary widely. I regularly pray for his wisdom and safety as he navigates this challenging landscape.

I fully expect major public health distractions—or multiple distractions—to try and derail this work. While healthier processed foods may emerge from reduced toxic chemicals in our food supply, they will never compare to nutritious whole foods. The enemy seeks to keep God's people sick, and the landscape of government and politics is unpredictable. Robert F. Kennedy, Jr. is not our savior—he would likely be the first to admit it. His position as Secretary of HHS is temporary, and his efforts could easily be undone by the next administration.

This uncertainty reminds us that our hope cannot rest on shifting policies or fallible human systems. As Scripture declares, *"I the Lord do not change"* (Malachi 3:6 *NIV*). Science and government will evolve, but *"Jesus Christ is the same yesterday and today and forever"* (Hebrews 13:8 *NIV*). This unchanging truth provides the foundation we need to honor our temples amid political shifts.

Ultimately, Kennedy cannot control what we choose to put into our bodies or how we care for ourselves; that sacred responsibility lies with each of us. Honoring our bodies is a task assigned by God—not by the government, politicians, or medical professionals.

As we look at the challenges facing our health and well-being in the following chapters, ponder these questions:

- How have societal norms, modern healthcare, and our food system shifted away from God's design for our bodies?
- In what ways have we conformed to a world that often prioritizes profit over health?

As you read through these topics, think about how you can align your choices with timeless biblical principles in a rapidly changing world.

CHAPTER 1

Redefining Normal: The Cost of Conformity

"It is no measure of health to be well adjusted to a profoundly sick society."

—Jiddu Krishnamurti,
Indian philosopher, speaker, and writer

Daniel and his friends— Shadrach, Meshach, and Abednego— were taken captive when King Nebuchadnezzar conquered Jerusalem. They were expected to conform to Babylonian customs— including its religious practices. When commanded to worship a golden idol, Shadrach, Meshach, and Abednego refused, declaring their trust in God. As a result, they were thrown into a fiery furnace. To the king's amazement, they emerged unharmed, accompanied by a mysterious fourth figure, "like a son of the gods." Their faithfulness led the king to praise their God and promote them.

As part of their training in the palace, Daniel and his friends were assigned the same rich food and wine as the other young men. The banquet hall overflowed with lavish meats, fine wines, and delicacies fit for royalty. But Daniel refused to defile his body with the king's food or wine. He pleaded with the official to let him and his friends eat vegetables and drink water.

Defying the king's orders was risky. So why did Daniel refuse to conform?

Bought at a Price

The apostle Paul reminds us, we are not our own and were bought at a price (1 Corinthians 6:19-20). Paul's words aren't about ownership in the worldly sense. They are about redemption - a divine transaction where Jesus paid the ultimate price for our freedom.

This redemption changes everything. We're no longer slaves to sin or bound by the world's standards. Instead, we're free to live as God intended. But with this freedom comes responsibility. We're called to honor God with our bodies, our choices, and our lives.

> *You are to be holy to me because I, the Lord, am holy, and I have set you apart from the nations to be my own.*

(Leviticus 20:26 *NIV*)

Being set apart doesn't mean withdrawing from the world. It means living in it differently in ways that honor His ownership and set an example for nonbelievers. This is a privilege – not just a responsibility.

Redefining Normal

A desire to fit in is part of human nature. We are wired for connection, and from childhood, society reinforces this instinct. We're encouraged to follow the crowd, conform to majority thinking, and believe that fitting in leads to happiness and acceptance.

The reality is that in our society the default state of "normal" is often one of chronic disease, mental health struggles, and poor overall health. In the United States, chronic conditions such as obesity, diabetes, and heart disease are widespread. More than 70% of adults are overweight or obese, and the rates of childhood obesity have tripled in recent decades. Mental health struggles, including but not limited to anxiety and depression, affect 23% of adults, and rates among children have risen significantly in recent years.

When I am told that my bloodwork is normal, or something is normal for my age, my response is, "I don't care to be normal. I want to be optimal."

We were created to be so much more than average. Each of us has been "fearfully and wonderfully made" with unique gifts to offer the world.

For you created my inmost being; you knit me together in my mother's womb. I praise you because I am fearfully and wonderfully made; your works are wonderful, I know that full well.

(Psalm 139:13-14 *NIV*)

So, I ask you—do you really want to be normal? Or do you want to be optimally healthy, fully alive, and unapologetically yourself?

The Average of 5: How Social Circles Influence Our Health

Choosing optimal health often means surrounding yourself with people who support that decision. Did you know your weight is significantly influenced by those you spend the most time with?

The people in our inner circle don't just impact our social lives—they shape our eating habits, exercise routines, and even our mindsets around wellness. Motivational speakers like Jim Rohn have popularized the idea that our lives reflect the average of the five people we spend the most time with, highlighting the profound influence of our social environment.

Research shows that obesity and health behaviors can spread through social networks. This gives new meaning to the phrase "it runs in the family"—as dietary and lifestyle habits tend to run in families.

Although genetics can make someone more susceptible to certain health challenges, the way a family lives and interacts often has a bigger effect. If you're raised in a home where unhealthy eating and inactivity are common, you're more likely to follow those habits as an adult, no matter your genes. On the other hand, families that focus on eating well, staying active, and maintaining strong social ties can overcome genetic risks.

As social creatures, we naturally want to fit in with our groups and may be influenced to adopt the habits and beliefs of those closest to us. If the people we spend most of our time with—including those in our faith communities—prefer unhealthy, processed foods and inactive lifestyles, these choices start to seem normal to us.

This conformity can lead to groupthink, where members of a group avoid critical thinking and different viewpoints in order to maintain harmony. Ignoring diverse perspectives and information can result in poor decisions and severe consequences. Groupthink within the medical community likely contributed to widespread overprescription of opioids. Despite emerging evidence of harm, the prevailing consensus delayed corrective action, leading to addiction and overdose deaths.

> *Each one should test their own actions. Then they can take pride in themselves alone, without comparing themselves to someone else.*
>
> (Galatians 6:4 *NIV*)

Understanding the influence of our closest connections is crucial to breaking free from unhealthy norms, even when it means challenging the status quo. Scripture reminds us of the value of mutual support and the power of community, as well as the importance of personal accountability.

> *Two are better than one, because they have a good return for their labor: If either of them falls down, one can help the other up. But pity anyone who falls and has no one to help them up. Also, if two lie down together, they will keep warm. But, how*

can one keep warm alone? Though one may be overpowered,
two can defend themselves. A cord of three strands is not
quickly broken.

(Ecclesiastes 4:9-12 *NIV*)

Surrounding ourselves with people who value health and faith makes all the difference. Joining or forming a group to study this book can create a supportive environment that nurtures healthy habits and spiritual growth.

But what does a community built around true health actually look like?

The Mediterranean Lifestyle

The Mediterranean diet is one of the most studied dietary patterns, but its health benefits extend beyond food. The Mediterranean way of life plays a significant role in the better health outcomes observed in the region.

Unlike modern Western habits, where meals are rushed, eaten alone, or consumed on the go, traditional Mediterranean cultures treat food as a slow, communal experience—one that fosters connection, gratitude, and joy. Meals are celebrations, not transactions. They are shared with family and friends gathered around the table, strengthening relationships and fostering a sense of belonging. Meals are enjoyed at a relaxed pace, paired with laughter, conversation, and presence.

In these regions, people tend to move naturally throughout the day. Rather than treating exercise as something separate, daily activity is integrated into life—walking to visit friends, working outdoors, or preparing food from scratch. Days follow a natural rhythm of work, rest, and worship. Even in the busiest seasons, time is intentionally carved out for family, faith, and fellowship.

This way of living is a stark contrast to the sedentary, stress-driven habits common in Western society—where convenience replaces connection, and eating is more about efficiency than enjoyment.

So rather than just asking, "What should I eat?" a better question might be: How should I live?

Food as Nourishment, Not Comfort or Reward

The Mediterranean lifestyle shows us how community, purpose, and healthy habits contribute to longer, happier lives. However, in many other places, our relationship with food is more complicated, often influenced by our emotions and psychological needs.

How we view food can lead to unhealthy eating behaviors, from binge eating under stress to using sugary treats as a reward or for emotional comfort. Participating in such habits reveals that we've lost touch with the original purpose of food as a nourishing gift from God. His bounty is intended to sustain and strengthen us, not to replace the genuine comfort and joy found in a deeper connection with Him.

Why do we fall into having an unhealthy relationship with food? Studies point to a mix of biological, psychological, and social factors.

Biologically, we're drawn to foods high in sugar, fat, and salt because they trigger our brain's reward center. Over time, we can start to crave these foods even when we're not hungry, leading to a cycle of craving and consumption driven more by the brain's demand for pleasure rather than the actual need for nourishment.

Psychologically, food can become a way to deal with difficult emotions, providing a temporary escape from stress, anxiety, or loneliness. It becomes a coping mechanism, rather than nourishment.

Socioculturally, the world around us encourages using food as a reward or comfort. Advertisements make unhealthy foods look really appealing, and it's not uncommon for parents to use treats to reward or console their kids. All of this reinforces the idea that food is for pleasure rather than nourishment.

Breaking free from deep-seated perceptions and emotional attachments to food requires courage. It doesn't mean we can't enjoy food. It means questioning what's considered normal and learning to see food as nourishment, rather than something to fill an emotional need. When we can do that, a sense of freedom opens to us—a space where we are nourished in both body and spirit, prepared to fulfill our divine calling.

Action Steps for Crafting a Path Forward

Having explored the impact of our social circles, the wisdom of the Mediterranean lifestyle, and our complicated relationship with food, it's clear that while there are challenges, there are also opportunities for positive change. Each concept—The Average of 5, the Mediterranean lifestyle, and viewing food as nourishment—offers actionable insights into improving our health and happiness. Let's look at how we can use these insights to create a life of balance, health, and purpose.

1. **Evaluate Your Average of 5:** The people you surround yourself with significantly influence your lifestyle choices.

   - List the five people you spend the most time with and note their influence on your health habits.
   - Look for communities and friends who value health and wellness; consider joining a fitness group, taking healthy cooking classes, or getting involved with a community garden.

I'm blessed to have friends who love healthy eating as much as I do, and we help each other deal with food allergies and sensitivities. Bringing like-minded people into your life can add to your current relationships and expand your circle of support.

2. **Embrace the Mediterranean Lifestyle Principles:** The Mediterranean way of life goes beyond just food—it's about balance, connection, and well-being. It emphasizes not only living longer, but also living well, with vibrant health and strong relationships. To embody these lessons in your daily life, consider the following action steps:

- Avoid eating on the go and share meals with loved ones as often as possible.
- Find ways to incorporate natural movement into your daily routine like walking, gardening, or cycling.
- Volunteer or join a local community group to foster strong social connections and community involvement.
- Find a sense of purpose and allocate time for relaxation and stress management.

3. **Rethink Food as Nourishment:** Shift your perspective on food from being a source of comfort or reward to nourishment for your body and soul.

- Practice mindful eating. This means making a conscious effort to change where and how we eat. I've found myself eating in the car or while distracted by the TV more times than I'd like to admit. By starting each meal with a moment of gratitude, being fully present, savoring each bite, and listening to our body's hunger and fullness cues, we can begin to appreciate food as nourishment.
- Develop healthy coping mechanisms. When emotions run high, seek out non-food ways to cope and deal with them rather than stuffing them. Consider prayer, journaling, talking with a friend, or going for a walk. Personally, I've discovered that listening to a sermon while working in the yard allows me to redirect my focus and find solace.

Choosing a different path isn't easy. Whether it's resisting unhealthy food habits, challenging societal expectations, or standing firm in faith, defying the norm requires courage. But as we have been promised, those who remain steadfast in their convictions are often rewarded—not just in physical health, but in spiritual and personal growth.

The Strength to Stand Apart

When Daniel and his friends refused the king's rich food and wine, they took a risk. The official in charge was concerned that if they appeared weaker than the other young men, it would reflect poorly on him. Initially, he refused, but Daniel talked him into a ten-day trial. At the end of those ten days, Daniel and his friends looked stronger and healthier than the others. Their obedience was honored, and they were allowed to continue their diet.

But this was only the beginning of Daniel's courageous stand. When King Darius was manipulated into outlawing prayer to anyone but himself, Daniel refused to comply. He was thrown into a den of lions for his defiance, but God miraculously protected him. The next morning, he emerged unharmed, and the king declared that all should worship the one true God. Daniel's story is a testament to the rewards of standing apart from the crowd and choosing what is right over what is easy.

Like Daniel, we face choices every day—choices about how we care for our bodies, what we eat, and who we surround ourselves with. The world's definition of *normal* is convenient but costly.

A New Normal: Embracing the Extraordinary

As we've explored the complex relationship between food, our social circles, and societal norms, it's natural to feel resistance. The path of nonconformity is rarely easy. Choosing to honor our bodies as sacred temples—rather than treating them as vessels for comfort, reward, or convenience—requires courage and perseverance.

Yet, the stakes have never been higher. The statistics are clear: our culture's definition of normal has led to epidemics of chronic disease, mental health struggles, and declining well-being. If we continue down this road, we risk not only our own health but also the legacy we leave for future generations.

What would it look like if we stepped away from the status quo? What if we dared to create a new normal—where food is nourishment, not an emotional crutch? Where we cultivate relationships that uplift and inspire us toward better health? Where we trust that the God who knit us together in our mother's womb has a better plan than the world's shallow definition of normal?

This transformation toward a new normal begins with our bodies—the sacred temples where the Holy Spirit dwells. By choosing nourishing food, meaningful relationships, and alignment with God's will, we honor these temples and unlock the path to true health.

It won't be easy. There will be loneliness, misunderstanding, and the temptation to give in to societal pressures. But as we've seen in Daniel's story and the enduring wisdom of Mediterranean lifestyle principles, the cost of nonconformity pales in comparison to the freedom, purpose, and abundant life that awaits on the other side.

Do not conform to the pattern of this world, but be transformed
by the renewing of your mind.

(Romans 12:2 *NIV*)

So, let's create a new normal—not defined by the world's standards, but by the transformative power of faith, community, and respect for the bodies we've been given. In this extraordinary journey, we can find the abundant life we truly seek.

The choice is yours. Will you follow the world's definition of normal—settling for chronic disease, exhaustion, and disconnection? Or will you, like Daniel, take a stand and choose a better way?

CHAPTER 2

Power and Profit:
The Shaping of Modern Healthcare

For what will it profit a man if he gains the
whole world, and loses his own soul?

(Mark 8:36 *NKJV*)

There was a time when doctors prioritized patient well-being over profit, when medicine was about healing, not business. It wasn't perfect, but it was personal—built upon relationships of trust rather than corporate interests.

Then, everything changed.

One man—one of the richest and most powerful figures in American history—saw an opportunity to reshape medicine for his own benefit. With unmatched financial influence, he set the stage for a monumental shift in healthcare, steering it away from its healing roots and toward an era dominated by profit and control.

Who was he? And how did he forever alter the course of modern medicine?

Medicine's Robber Baron

At the turn of the 20th century, industrial tycoons controlled the American economy, amassing incredible wealth and power. Among them was a man whose name became synonymous with money, influence, and ruthless business tactics—a man whose empire extended far beyond his original industry, reaching into education, healthcare, and even the way we view medicine itself.

His fortune was built on oil—an industry he monopolized with an iron grip, controlling everything from drilling to delivery. He colluded with the railroad to control shipping costs, crushing competitors through price wars until they had no choice but to surrender or sell their businesses to him.

And then, with his monopoly secured, he turned his sights on a new frontier—medicine. His mission? To make petroleum-based pharmaceuticals the foundation of modern medicine.

At the time, natural remedies, herbal medicine, and holistic healing were common practice. But for this titan of industry, those approaches didn't offer the level of profit he was looking for. If medicine could be controlled—if pharmaceutical drugs could become the standard of care—it would create an entirely new market, one where oil-based chemicals could be sold not just as fuel, but as medicine.

And so, the plan was set in motion.

To make it work, he needed a way to reshape medical education, to convince the world that his version of medicine was the only version that mattered. His key tool in this transformation was a highly influential report that would dictate the future of healthcare.

Medicine Redefined: Flexner's Legacy

Published in 1910 as an effort to improve education, the report evaluated medical schools across the United States and Canada. The report pushed for a uniform, science-based approach to medical education, with professors focused on full-time research and instruction. In reality, this report eliminated competition and reshaped medicine in favor of a single model—one built on pharmaceuticals and standardization.

One of the report's more controversial outcomes was its condemnation of schools teaching natural or alternative medicine. Branded as unscientific, these schools were systematically defunded and eliminated, sidelining generations of healing traditions. This resulted in a medical system where pharmaceutical-based care became the gold standard, and where alternative medicine was dismissed, ridiculed, or outright banned.

By now, you may have figured out who was behind this transformation.

His name? John D. Rockefeller. The report? *The Flexner Report.*

Rockefeller's influence didn't just fund medical schools—it shaped the entire direction of healthcare. By controlling the funding, he ensured that only the medical institutions aligned with his vision survived.

Even a century later, the consequences of this shift are still felt. In a 2011 reflection marking 100 years since the report, Thomas Duffy, MD noted that the shift toward a research-focused medical culture downplayed the importance of hands-on patient care, practice-based wisdom, and compassion. He argued that this transformation has undermined the trust and respect once held for the medical profession.

The focus of modern medical education remains heavily skewed toward pharmaceuticals, leaving little room for studying nutrition or alternative treatments. Although we're told to consult a doctor before making dietary changes, most medical students receive only a few hours of nutrition training. Without exposure to natural treatments, doctors are unlikely to suggest them, even though natural substances like curcumin or omega-3s have been shown to rival pharmaceutical drugs in effectiveness.

The rift between conventional and alternative medicine remains, a direct consequence of Rockefeller's medical empire and *The Flexner Report's* legacy.

Turf Wars in Healthcare: The AMA's Battle Against Chiropractic Care

In 1987, the American Medical Association (AMA) sparked a turf war with chiropractors, leading to a landmark lawsuit called Wilk v. AMA. This legal battle shed light on the AMA's efforts to undermine chiropractic care, revealing a campaign of misinformation and boycotts against chiropractors.

The settlement marked a significant victory for chiropractors and a turning point for alternative medicine. It demonstrated the lengths traditional medical institutions would go to maintain their dominance. The documentary *Doctored* further explores this conflict, showing how financial interests have often driven opposition to alternative and complementary medicine practices.

The AND's Push for Dietary Dominance

Likewise, the Academy of Nutrition and Dietetics (AND) continually lobbies for laws giving registered dietitians a monopoly on the right to offer nutritional advice. They've succeeded in some states, shutting down other nutrition experts and restricting people's access to diverse, independent dietary advice.

A revealing article was published by *The Cambridge University Press* in October 2022, exposing the AND's financial ties to food and beverage companies. Titled, The corporate capture of the nutrition profession in the USA: the case of the Academy of Nutrition and Dietetics, the article detailed these connections.

From 2011 to 2017, the AND accepted over $4 million from companies that make ultra-processed foods, soda, and other sugary foods, including Conagra, Coca-Cola, PepsiCo, Nestlé, Kellogg's, and Hershey. These are some of the same companies sponsoring booths and continuing education at the AND conferences.

The AND's industry ties and push for greater control raise serious concerns. Unlike other professions, dietitian licensure requires paid AND membership. Physicians, for example, aren't required to join the American Medical Association. Tying licensure to an organization with deep industry connections and influence over nutrition policy is problematic.

These examples show the ongoing turf wars in healthcare, where money and power sometimes matter more than patients' needs and choices. *The Flexner Report's* impact, along with the actions of the AMA and the AND, reveals a healthcare system with internal problems.

As we move into the next section, we'll look at how money and power also affect scientific studies and the journals that publish them.

Science for Sale

Peer-reviewed medical journals have long been trusted sources of scientific information. But the pharmaceutical industry's influence has compromised the integrity of research and journal articles. Many journals rely on industry funding, raising concerns about bias in published research.

Catherine DeAngelis, MD, former editor-in-chief of the *Journal of the American Medical Association (JAMA)*, spoke out against aggressive pressure from drug advertisers to influence content. After resigning in 2011, she told National Public Radio (NPR) she felt ongoing pressure to compromise editorial integrity to maintain advertising revenue.

In a 2008 lecture, Dr. DeAngelis warned that pharmaceutical and biotech companies, especially their marketing divisions, wield significant influence over medical research. Their deep financial backing often pushes scientists into ethically questionable positions, leading to biased research that prioritizes profit over truth.

Pharmaceutical company influence on researchers can take various forms, such as the following:

- **Speakers' bureau.** Drug companies can pay researchers to travel, sometimes in luxury, to various events to deliver speeches and show slides prepared by the company. The companies may also sponsor medical conferences where company representatives have a role in selecting the speakers and topics presented.
- **Ghostwriting.** In some cases, a company will write an article and pay a scientist to claim authorship and submit it to a scientific journal, a practice known as ghostwriting.
- **Consulting.** Additionally, companies may hire researchers for consulting, seeking not just their expertise but also their reputable names to boost the company's image.

Another concern is how researchers can design studies to get the results they want. They don't have to share failed studies and only share the successful ones with the FDA and journals. This selective reporting can make treatments seem safer or better than they really are, leaving doctors and patients without all the facts.

Pharmaceutical companies further influence research by funding medical journals—not just through advertising, but by paying journals to print extra copies of studies that favor their drugs. This financial relationship may make journals more likely to publish positive studies while rejecting or delaying negative ones. Even after editorial and peer review, these companies can pressure journals to retract articles that don't align with their interests.

We saw this firsthand with the retractions of two hydroxychloroquine papers published in *The Lancet* and *The New England Journal of Medicine* during the COVID-19 pandemic. The same authors wrote both papers, and their removal raised serious concerns about research integrity, whether biased interests were at play, and the implications for public health.

This issue isn't limited to pharmaceuticals. Some nutrition studies are also designed to minimize positive effects or prevent them from outperforming drugs. Researchers might use poorly absorbed nutrient forms or doses too low to be effective. A stark example of study manipulation occurred in the UK's RECOVERY Trial, where COVID-19 patients received fatal doses of hydroxychloroquine, leading researchers to conclude it didn't lower the risk of death.

The politicization of hydroxychloroquine and media narratives linked to anti-Trump sentiment further complicated the situation. While proving specific motives is difficult, some speculate these studies were published to discredit hydroxychloroquine. This may have helped preserve Emergency Use Authorization (EUA) for experimental treatments, since EUA cannot be granted if a viable treatment exists. The handling of hydroxychloroquine research raises broader concerns about transparency in scientific publishing.

These patterns—selective reporting, financial influence, and political bias—all contribute to a growing public distrust in scientific research, especially during times of crisis. Understanding these dynamics is critical in discerning which studies are truly reliable and which may be skewed by external agendas.

Censorship of Doctors and Researchers

The influence of money and power on scientific research leads to a troubling issue: censorship of medical professionals and researchers who challenge the status quo. Their voices are often silenced, reputations attacked, and work dismissed, hindering scientific progress.

Einstein said, "Unthinking respect for authority is the greatest enemy of truth." Pioneers like Newton, Copernicus, Pasteur, and Lister defied established beliefs at great personal cost. Ignaz Semmelweis, who suggested doctors wash hands between patients, faced harsh criticism and rejection. Just as Jesus was rejected, these innovators were ridiculed and ostracized—yet their courage led to world-changing breakthroughs.

True science is never "settled". It thrives on debate and adaptation, not censorship. Dissenting voices questioning pharmaceuticals, nutrition guidelines, or medical interventions are often labeled as misinformation, regardless of evidence. When debate is shut down, we risk repeating history's mistakes.

Many once accepted medical practices were later proven harmful. For example, removing parts of the brain to treat mental illness, and using X-rays and thalidomide for pregnant women led to devastating birth defects. Karo syrup and powdered milk were once promoted over breastmilk. Without challengers, we might still use arsenic for arthritis or practice bloodletting.

Suppressing ideas hinders progress and puts lives at risk. Maintaining scientific integrity and public trust requires keeping medical information open and free from external influences, whether it's the pharmaceutical industry, media, or government. Science should remain a process of constant questioning, not a tool for control or censorship.

Regulatory Capture and Corruption: A Biblical Lens

*"The care of human life and happiness, and not
their destruction, is the first and only legitimate
object of good government."*

—Thomas Jefferson

The Bible is filled with warnings about corruption, from the era of the judges to the Pharisees, teaching us to be discerning and not to place our trust in earthly powers. As Ecclesiastes 1:9 (*CSB*) reminds us, *"What has been is what will be, and what has been done is what will be done; there is nothing new under the sun,"* including the corruption of those in authority.

Today, we see this biblical truth reflected in regulatory capture. Agencies like the Food and Drug Administration (FDA) and Environmental Protection Agency (EPA)—meant to protect public health—are influenced by the industries they oversee. This influence has led to weak regulations and the approval of harmful drugs and devices linked to serious health issues and even death.

Essure was marketed as a safe, permanent birth control device but left thousands of women with debilitating pain, organ damage, and auto-immune reactions before it was finally pulled from the market. Vioxx, a widely used painkiller, was recalled after being linked to thousands of fatal heart attacks and strokes. Glyphosate-containing products like Roundup® remain on the market despite mounting evidence tying them to cancer and environmental harm.

The Centers for Disease Control and Prevention (CDC) also faces conflicts of interest, accepting outside funding and allowing scientists to earn royalties. This raises serious concerns about integrity and its impact on public health. As chronic diseases rise and life expectancy plateaus, these agencies continue to fall short in their mission to improve health outcomes.

As Christians, we have a duty to be vigilant, do our own research, and place our trust in God rather than in fallible human institutions. Watchdog groups work to expose corruption, but their findings are often ignored by mainstream media. We must heed the warning:

> *Beware of false prophets, who come to you in sheep's clothing but inwardly they are ravenous wolves.*

(Matthew 7:15 *NKJV*)

Corporate Medicine's Heavy Toll

In recent years, corporations have been buying up medical practices, turning practitioners into employees, and changing how healthcare operates. Instead of making their own decisions regarding patient care, practitioners are directed by protocols and profit-driven agendas imposed by insurance companies and corporate administrators.

As a result, practitioners face increasing pressure and challenges. They have limited time with each patient and spend considerable time preparing and writing chart notes for each visit. They must follow standardized treatment protocols that may not suit individual patient needs. Moreover, corporate medicine has led to a focus on cost control and efficiency, sometimes at the expense of personalized and comprehensive care. All this pressure is taking a toll on doctors, leading to alarming rates of burnout and suicide among physicians.

Corporate medicine has altered the doctor-patient relationship, diminishing trust and collaboration as doctors navigate the tension between corporate profits and patient care. This shift has also compromised the practice of informed consent, an ethical and legal obligation for providers. Informed consent requires giving patients all the information they need about their treatment options to make an informed decision. However, due to time constraints and competing demands, informed consent is often overlooked or ignored.

Healthcare has become more efficient in some ways, but at a cost. The system now prioritizes profit and bureaucracy over true healing, leaving both doctors and patients struggling within its constraints.

Action Steps to Reclaim the Sanctity of Healthcare

The transformation of our healthcare system has had profound consequences, but change doesn't happen through passive observation. Each of us has the power to advocate for a system that truly serves its purpose—one that prioritizes patient care, medical integrity, and holistic well-being. The following steps will help you take informed, meaningful action in reclaiming the true sanctity of your healthcare.

1. **Educate Yourself:** Learn how to research medical information by using reliable sources like PubMed. This is a free search engine provided by the National Institutes of Health (NIH), which is a part of the United States Department of Health and Human Services. It's one of the largest and most trusted databases for medical and scientific research worldwide.

2. **Stay Informed:** Stay updated on healthcare issues and advancements by following reputable sources (see the Resources for current sources).

3. **Advocate for Informed Consent:** Ensure that you and your family members have a say in your healthcare decisions. Have open discussions with healthcare providers to fully understand your treatment options and any associated risks.

4. **Stay Engaged:** Take an active role in your healthcare by participating in discussions with your healthcare team and asking questions about your treatment plan.

5. **Find a New Practitioner:** If you're not happy with your practitioner or prefer a more natural approach, and have expressed your concerns to no avail, find another practitioner. It's not easy

establishing a new relationship, but you are not obligated to accept poor care or communication.

6. **Pray and Seek Guidance:** Pray for wisdom and discernment in navigating healthcare decisions and seek guidance from a trusted advisor.

Reclaiming Healthcare's True Purpose

The consequences of one man's vision still shape healthcare today. Rockefeller's calculated takeover of medicine led to a system where pharmaceutical interests dominate medical education, natural healing methods, and prioritize corporate profits over patient care.

The Flexner Report dismantled medical diversity, leading to a one-size-fits-all approach prioritizing pharmaceuticals over holistic healing. The AMA and pharmaceutical industry continue this trend, creating a system where questioning the norm is met with hostility, and alternatives are suppressed and tied up in red tape.

True healing doesn't come from fallible institutions but from divine wisdom and personal responsibility. Scripture reminds us: *"Don't put your confidence in powerful people; there is no help for you there"* (Psalm 146:3 *NLT*).

Never underestimate the power of individual action. The Bible and history remind us that ordinary people can create extraordinary change. By educating ourselves, advocating for informed consent, and seeking divine guidance, each of us can help reshape the future of healthcare.

CHAPTER 3

How Our Food Went from Whole to Ultra-Processed

"Let food be thy medicine and medicine be thy food."

—Hippocrates

Step back in time with me and meet Betty, a happy homemaker that enjoyed cooking and caring for her family, until World War II changed everything. With her husband off at war, Betty answered the call to work, encouraged by government ads praising women's contributions.

At first, Betty missed her kitchen and family, but she soon grew to love her job. She enjoyed the independence, camaraderie, and sense of purpose. However, when the war ended, her husband expected things to return to normal, with Betty back at home.

But life was different. Many women, including Betty, weren't ready to give up their jobs. Yet, balancing work and family proved exhausting. Time in the kitchen became a burden.

Then came the seemingly perfect solution: canned goods, frozen meals, boxed dinners—modern conveniences promising to save time without sacrificing quality. Betty embraced these processed foods eagerly. Cooking became quicker, meals were easier, and life seemed to be in perfect balance.

But over time, things started to change.

Her family, once full of energy, started feeling sluggish. The kids were sick frequently, and the pounds crept on. The joy of food—the aromas, the flavors, the connection around the table—began to fade.

Something was different. But Betty wasn't sure what.

What Happened to Our Food?

It was just a century ago when kitchens were filled with the rich aromas of hearty stews simmering on cast-iron stoves and freshly baked pies cooling on windowsills. Today, the pervasive smell of fast food lingering in the car is more common than the smell of home-cooked meals.

This stark contrast mirrors the profound transformation of our food system—a shift away from the nutrient-rich whole foods that sustained our ancestors to a diet dominated by ultra-processed foods (UPFs), or food-like products. We've reached the point where over 73% of the U.S. food supply is UPFs.

In the previous chapter, we explored how the medical industry succumbed to power and greed. Now, we turn to another critical area of health that has drifted from God's design: our food. This chapter will expose the dramatic shifts from natural, ancestral farming to today's chemically driven food production.

We'll dive into the industrialization of food, the influence of large corporations, and how regulatory agencies like the EPA, FDA, and USDA have swayed from their original missions. Additionally, we'll explore the consequences of these changes on our health and what Scripture teaches about the food we eat.

Hippocrates, the ancient Greek physician hailed as the "father of medicine," famously advised, "Let food be thy medicine and medicine be thy food." Our ancestors understood that the foods God gave us were meant to nourish, sustain, and heal. Today they would hardly recognize the food we consume: UPFs packed with empty calories and artificial ingredients fueling disease more than health.

We can't ignore the link between our diet and the skyrocketing rates of chronic diseases like diabetes, autoimmune disorders, and heart disease. Our genes haven't changed much over time, but our food has.

To understand how we reached this point, we need to take a historical journey through the industrialization of food and answer a crucial question:

What happened to our food?

The Evolution of Processed Foods: From Necessity to Excess

WWII was a turning point for the American diet. During the war, food rationing and government ads pushing margarine as a healthy alternative to scarce butter changed what people ate. After the war, there was a large shift away from meals made with home-grown ingredients to eating more UPFs. At the same time, traditional methods of food preservation, like drying, smoking, and canning, started to be replaced by new industrial methods that often reduce food's nutritional value.

Post WWII, the grocery industry boomed. Imagine stepping into a supermarket at this time. It's compact, stocked with essentials like fresh fruits, vegetables, grains, a meat counter, and just a few canned and dairy products. Now, picture today's supermarket. Frozen meals, snacks, sugary drinks, and aisles of processed foods fill most of the space, with fresh, whole foods pushed to the perimeter.

U.S. government subsidies have partially driven this shift by favoring crops like corn, soy, wheat, and rice—key ingredients in UPFs. Despite recommendations for a fruit and vegetable-rich diet, these healthier options receive fewer subsidies. This subsidy system masks the true economic costs, as well as the health and environmental costs of UPFs, making whole foods seem more expensive.

Beyond the nutritional concerns associated with UPFs, the widespread use of food additives compounds health risks. UPFs contribute to chronic inflammatory diseases (e.g., obesity, diabetes, heart disease, certain cancers, etc.). UPFs typically contain up to 500 times more salt than home-cooked meals, significantly increasing the risk of excessive sodium intake.

The Hidden Dangers of Food Additives

Food additives are used to enhance flavor, texture, shelf life, and appearance, but research has linked several to concerning health effects. Not all additives within a category are necessarily linked to every listed effect, but the cumulative impact of regular exposure is worth examining. Below are some of the most common additives and their potential health risks:

- **Artificial Sweeteners** (saccharin, sucralose, aspartame, erythritol, sorbitol): Altered gut microbiota, increased intestinal permeability, increased oxidative stress and inflammation, insulin resistance, weight gain, increased risk of diabetes, cardiovascular disease, stroke, depression, and immune system disruption.

- **Emulsifiers** (mono- and diglycerides, carrageenan, cellulose gum, carboxymethyl cellulose, polysorbate 80, soy lecithin, sodium alginate): Increased cancer risk, altered gut microbiota, bacterial translocation across the gut lining, increased food intake, inflammation, obesity, and immune dysfunction.

- **Artificial Colors** (Red 40, Yellow 5, Yellow 6): Hyperactivity/ attention deficit and neurobehavioral effects in children, allergic reactions, immune system dysregulation, and increased cancer risk.

- **Preservatives** (sulfites, butylated hydroxyanisole or BHA, benzoates, propylparaben, potassium bromate): Birth defects in mice, hyperactive behavior in children, headaches, altered gut microbiota, allergic reactions, increased cancer risk, oxidative stress, inflammation, DNA damage, neurotoxicity, estrogenic effects, obesity, and impaired immune function.

- **Excitotoxins** (MSG, L-glutamate, aspartate): Toxicity of the nervous and cardiovascular systems, gut microbiota disruption, insulin resistance, inflammation, metabolic disturbances, oxidative stress, and increased risk of neurodegenerative disorders.

- **Salt** (sodium chloride): In excess, increased risk of high blood pressure, cardiovascular disease, stroke, kidney problems; exacerbation of autoimmune conditions; oxidative stress; and acidifying effect on the body.

While natural salts (e.g., sea salt, Himalayan salt) contain trace minerals and are generally preferable to table salt, excessive intake of any salt can be problematic. The chloride component in salt has an acidifying effect on the body. Those who are sodium-sensitive may experience more pronounced health issues from high salt consumption.

Many of these additives are deemed Generally Recognized as Safe (GRAS) by the FDA, often without extensive testing for their long-term effects. Combined with high levels of added sugars, unhealthy fats, and salt in UPFs, additives pose significant health risks for consumers.

In March 2025, RFK Jr., as HHS Secretary, directed the FDA to explore closing the GRAS pathway—a loophole letting companies self-affirm ingredient safety without independent review. While this move seeks to increase transparency and protect public health, its fate and permanency are uncertain.

A more recent GRAS-approved food modification is Apeel®, a coating applied to fresh produce to extend shelf life and reduce food waste. Apeel is derived from highly processed seed oils. Through chemical processing, these oils are converted into mono- and diglycerides—the same emulsifiers commonly used in processed food.

The coating process involves the use of solvents and may contain trace amounts of heavy metals. Unlike traditional wax coatings that can be scrubbed off, Apeel forms an invisible barrier that cannot be completely removed.

Adding to concerns, Apeel and its organic counterpart, Organipeel®, contain undisclosed "proprietary" ingredients. In the U.S., produce treated with these coatings is not required to be labeled, leaving consumers unable to make fully informed choices about what they're eating. Even certified organic produce can be coated, making this yet another example of how industrial food processing continues to interfere with nature under the guise of innovation.

Food industry trends have long prioritized taste and profit over health. In the 1970s, when the USDA advised against eating fat, manufacturers reformulated products. They removed fat but replaced it with added sugar and salt to compensate for lost flavor. The result? Consumers got sicker and fatter.

The Addictive Nature of Ultra-Processed Foods

Today, food companies employ engineers to create products that hit a "bliss point," making them irresistibly addictive. Marketers reinforce this with slogans like Lay's Potato Chips' "No one can eat just one." This calculated manipulation exploits the brain's reward system, driving us to want more.

Scientific evidence confirms that UPFs trigger brain responses similar to those caused by nicotine and alcohol. Consuming UPFs leads to a rapid blood sugar spike, flooding the brain with dopamine and creating feelings of pleasure. Over time, this can desensitize the brain, requiring more of these foods to achieve the same satisfaction.

This blood sugar-dopamine cycle leads to mood swings and intense cravings. It can also result in compulsive eating behaviors. Research links UPFs to binge eating, particularly in those vulnerable to eating disorders. Because UPFs are engineered for maximum palatability, they increase the likelihood of loss-of-control eating episodes, reinforcing addictive cycles.

Binge eating—defined as consuming large amounts of food in a short period, often with a sense of loss of control—strengthens food addiction and contributes to weight gain, metabolic dysfunction, and emotional distress. Studies confirm that UPFs make binge eating more likely by encouraging overeating beyond physical hunger due to their hyper-palatable nature.

Spiritual and Moral Implications

While food companies may not intend to lead us into sin, their profit-driven focus has created addictive, ultra-processed products that many experts consider psychoactive. The consumption of these substances can contribute to other mental health issues, such as anxiety and depression, in addition to compulsive eating behaviors and binge eating disorders. The Bible warns us against being ruled by cravings, urging discipline and self-control in all aspects of life.

> Do not love this world nor the things it offers you, for when you love the world, you do not have the love of the Father in you. For the world offers only a craving for physical pleasure, a craving for everything we see, and pride in our achievements and possessions. These are not from the Father, but are from this world.

(1 John 2:15-17 *NLT*)

In the next chapter, we'll examine gluttony—not just as a personal failing, but as a struggle made harder by the world we live in.

With the food industry putting profits before public health, we must be intentional about choosing nutrient-rich whole foods over processed ones. Understanding where our food comes from and how it's grown are also key to making wise, God-honoring choices.

The Evolution of Agriculture: Tracing the Nutrient Decline in Our Food

As our diets have shifted more towards processed foods, farming has also changed significantly. Before WWII, farmers worked with nature to keep the soil healthy, using organic methods rather than chemicals. They grew a wide variety of fruits and vegetables, including thousands of potato and apple varieties.

Farmers practiced crop rotation, composted, and found natural ways to manage pests. Soils were fertile, with more than 17 nutrients, and a complex underground ecosystem of microbes, earthworms, and fungi. They saved and cleaned their own seeds and shared them with neighbors. 'Hybridization' of plants happened naturally or intentionally when farmers planted their crop near a wild variety, hoping for more disease and pest-resistant plants.

This ancient wisdom aligns with biblical teachings on stewardship, emphasizing our duty to care for creation. God has entrusted us with protecting His gifts of diverse life and maintaining a healthy ecosystem for future generations. Genesis 2:15 reminds us that God gave humans a perfect world to care for and maintain. Leviticus 25:23 reminds us that the land is God's, and He has placed us as its caretakers.

The Lord God placed the man in the Garden of Eden
to tend and watch over it.

(Genesis 2:15 *NLT*)

*The land must never be sold on a permanent basis, for the
land belongs to me. You are only foreigners and tenant farmers
working for me.*

(Leviticus 25:23 *NLT*)

Since 1900, we've lost 75% of agricultural crop diversity, which is important for both variety and disease protection. Over time, natural and regenerative farming gave way to industrialized agriculture. Monoculture farming replaced diverse crops. Synthetic chemicals became the norm. Soil, once alive with nutrients, became depleted.

This shift accelerated dramatically after World War II, ushering in a new era of chemical-dependent farming that forever changed the quality of our food.

Repurposing Post-World War II Chemicals in Agriculture

During World War II, few farmworkers were available, so the government encouraged using tractors, fertilizers, and pesticides for efficiency and larger crop yields. After the war, chemical companies repurposed their military surplus and production capacity for agriculture.

One notorious example was the use of dichlorodiphenyltrichloroethane (DDT), once celebrated as a pest control miracle and advertised as "DDT is good for me." Its environmental and health dangers eventually came to light, leading to widespread bans. Meanwhile, pesticide overuse led to the development of resistant pests, requiring ever-more toxic chemicals.

Synthetic nitrogen fertilizers, made through methods like those used for explosives, offered a cheap but incomplete source of nutrients for plants. Combined with the use of machinery in farming, this led to the growth of monoculture practices and the loss of diversity.

Glyphosate, GMOs, and the Erosion of Soil and Human Health

Another chemical of concern is glyphosate, the active ingredient in the commonly used herbicide Roundup®. The EPA reports its use on nearly 300 million acres of U.S. cropland annually. The percentage of total crop acreage treated with glyphosate varies by crop:

1. Sugar beets: 98%
2. Soybeans: 92%
3. Cotton: 89%
4. Corn: 80%
5. Sunflowers: 74%
6. Spring wheat: 41%
7. Winter wheat: 20%

The FDA has detected glyphosate residues in various foods, including very high levels in chickpeas, lentils, oats, beans, and other grains.

Glyphosate, which was patented as an antibiotic, harms soil health by killing beneficial microorganisms and contributing to herbicide-resistant weeds. It works by blocking an essential enzyme in the shikimate pathway, which bacteria, fungi, and plants rely on to produce key amino acids necessary for growth and survival. While this pathway doesn't exist in humans, it is critical for gut bacteria that support digestion, immunity, and overall health.

The introduction of genetically modified organisms (GMOs) has fueled the expansion of monoculture crops, particularly those engineered to withstand glyphosate. As the active ingredient in Roundup, the world's most widely used herbicide, glyphosate use has sharply increased as a result of this expansion.

Genetic engineering (GE) differs vastly from traditional breeding or hybridization, which cross-pollinates within a species. Instead, GE inserts genes from other organisms—sometimes entirely different species—to create traits like herbicide resistance. During this process, genetically modified cells are often bathed in antibiotics to isolate resilient cells, raising concerns about antibiotic resistance.

As concerns about the health risks of GMOs and glyphosate grow, the industries behind them continue to challenge safety critiques. In 2015, the World Health Organization (WHO) classified glyphosate as a probable carcinogen. Since then, Bayer®, which acquired Monsanto—the developer of Roundup—has lost and settled numerous lawsuits from individuals who developed cancer after exposure to the herbicide.

Meanwhile, the FDA and EPA, tasked with protecting public health and the environment, have been criticized for endorsing glyphosate and GMOs, raising questions about industry influence over regulatory decisions. While the U.S. maintains near-unchecked acceptance of these products, other countries have imposed bans or strict regulations.

The EPA's allowable glyphosate residue limits are significantly higher than those in the European Union (EU)—often by a factor of 10 to 200. For example, while the EU enforces a default limit of 0.1 mg/kg, the U.S. permits up to 30 mg/kg in oats and 20 mg/kg in soybeans, corn, and wheat.

This regulatory approach highlights broader concerns about food safety and environmental sustainability as we examine the reliance on synthetic fertilizers and the resulting decline in crop nutrient content.

Diminishing Returns: The Decline of Soil Health and Food Nutrients

The widespread use of glyphosate and synthetic fertilizers—which mainly replenish nitrogen, phosphorus, and potassium (NPK)—has depleted the soil and reduced essential minerals. While NPK fuels plant growth, other nutrients like iron, zinc, and copper are equally vital for plant health and disease resistance. Modern farming practices have diminished these nutrients, impacting food quality and human health. Glyphosate worsens the issue by binding minerals like calcium, magnesium, manganese, and zinc, making them less available to plants.

From 1975 to 1997, nutrients in our produce declined significantly. Net changes in nutrient decline include:

- Calcium : 28.9% in fruit and 26.5% in vegetables.
- Iron: 16.4% in fruit and 36.1% in vegetables.
- Vitamin A: 16.4% in fruit and 21.4% in vegetables
- Vitamin D: 1.9% in fruit and 29.9% in vegetables

The drop in nutrients is connected to poor soil health and growing crops that provide the highest yields. Although modern farming produces more calories per acre, those calories are less nutritious, which means we have to eat more to get the same amount of nutrients.

Putting Biblical Stewardship into Action for a Healthier Tomorrow

We must return to regenerative and organic farming for a healthier future. These methods can produce as much or more than traditional farming under the right conditions. Focusing on soil health and plant diversity makes environmental challenges like drought easier to handle and uses fewer chemicals. These farming practices also better align with biblical stewardship of God's creation.

By prioritizing whole, nutrient-dense foods and supporting local organic farmers, we can influence production towards healthier options.

This honors our bodies as temples and respects what God created. Practical steps include:

- **Choosing Whole Foods:** Prioritize unprocessed, nutrient-rich foods.

- **Educating Yourself:** Learn about GMOs, regenerative agriculture, and organic farming.

- **Gardening, If Possible:** Grow your produce, even in small pots or a community garden.

- **Supporting Local and Organic:** Buy from local organic farmers and CSAs who don't use Organipeel. Choose heirloom varieties when possible.

- **Advocating for Change:** Support policies promoting regenerative farming and stricter food safety. Get involved in advocacy work.

- **Practicing Mindful Eating:** Make conscious choices about food quality and source.

Small, intentional choices can lead to lasting transformation. By focusing on whole foods and biblical stewardship, we can reclaim our health and food system integrity.

But what does this look like in everyday life? Let's return to Betty's story.

Lessons from Betty's Kitchen

Betty believed she had found the perfect balance—a way to keep her job and provide for her family. Processed foods seemed like a miracle. But over time, she saw what they took away from her family.

The energy, the health, the connection around the table—it had all slowly faded.

53

One evening, while stirring a prepackaged mix on the stove, she caught a familiar scent coming from outside—her neighbor's home-cooked stew simmering on the stove. It smelled rich, nourishing, real.

For the first time, Betty wondered: had she traded something truly valuable for mere convenience?

Betty and her husband negotiated a compromise. She wouldn't have to return to the kitchen full-time, but they would prioritize real food again. Processed meals would be an occasional convenience—not the foundation of their diet.

While Betty's story is fictional, her dilemma is real.

Reclaiming Our Food and Our Future

Many of us, like Betty, have been sold the illusion of convenience, only to wake up one day feeling disconnected from our food, our health, and our traditions. We live in a world where processed foods dominate our plates, our grocery stores, and our habits.

The good news? It's not too late.

We can reclaim what was lost—not by abandoning modern life, but by making intentional choices. When we choose whole, nourishing food, we are reclaiming our health and honoring the way God designed our bodies to thrive.

Our choices affect more than just our own well-being. The way we source and consume food impacts the land, the farmers, and the communities that sustain us. Every decision we make about food is an act of stewardship, reflecting our role as caretakers of God's creation.

The earth is the Lord's, and everything in it.

(Psalm 24:1 *NLT*)

Our modern food system encourages excess, waste, and disconnection from the land, but we have the power to push back. By choosing real, nutrient-dense food, supporting local farmers, and reducing reliance on ultra-processed convenience, we take a stand for health, sustainability, and faith-driven stewardship.

So, let me ask you:

What would happen if we brought real food back into our kitchens?

How would our health, our families, and even our faith be different if we chose nourishment over convenience?

The decision, just like Betty's, is ours to make.

CHAPTER 4

Beyond Moderation: Conquering Gluttony in a Super-Sized World

Their destiny is destruction, their god is their stomach, and their glory is in their shame. Their mind is set on earthly things.

(Philippians 3:19 *NIV*)

A favorite story from my childhood was *Mr. Grabbit the Rabbit*. Its message was so powerful that I later read it to my children. When I had grandchildren, I sought out a used copy of this out-of-print gem to share with them.

A Rabbit's Greed and Gluttony

Mr. Grabbit, a rabbit with an insatiable appetite for more, lives in a house overflowing with excess. He has piles of shoes, coats, hats, and even toothbrushes. His cellar is stuffed with more vegetables than he could ever eat. His bed is so laden with blankets and pillows that he struggles to find his way out each morning.

Mr. Grabbit's greed and gluttony leads him into a series of misadventures. He pushes others aside at the market for the biggest vegetables, drinks all the milkman's supply, and buys more coats and hats than he could ever wear. Finally, his impulse to take four umbrellas on a rainy day, causes him to be swept away by the wind and stranded atop a church steeple.

Biblical Lessons on Gluttony

Mr. Grabbit's story reflects a deeper truth about human nature. In the Garden of Eden, Adam and Eve were surrounded by abundance. They had everything they needed to live in perfect communion with God. However, Satan tempted them to indulge in the one thing they were told to avoid: the fruit from the Tree of Knowledge. He convinced Eve that eating the forbidden fruit would make her wise, not bring death as God had told them.

When Adam and Eve ate the forbidden fruit, they broke the rule God set for their good. This wasn't about feeding hunger. They desired more than what God had provided—they craved more knowledge and power, thinking it would bring more satisfaction. But by taking what they didn't need, they experienced shame and fear. They were forced to leave the Garden of Eden, and they lost what they needed most: their close, trusting relationship with God. (Genesis 3:1-24)

One of Satan's oldest lies is that indulgence won't harm us, but that it will set us free. After being delivered from Egypt, a group of Israelites complained about the lack of variety in the manna God had provided for them. They wanted to go back to Egypt for the "free" meat they ate as slaves, which wasn't free at all (Exodus 16:1-36).

Their willingness to give up freedom wasn't about need. It was about satisfying a craving. They wept in their discontent, causing Moses great distress. In response, God sent them quail driven in from the sea. The Israelites gathered excessively, with no one collecting less than ten homers (about 50 bushels). But as they gorged themselves, the Lord's anger flared, and many died with the meat still in their mouths.

The place where they were buried was called Kibroth-hattaavah, "the graves of craving." (Numbers 11:4-6, 31-34)

The Real Cost of Gluttony

What powerful lessons on desire and ingratitude—from Mr. Grab-bit's excesses to Adam and Eve's disobedience to the Israelites' craving for more. Each story shows how seeking beyond what is needed leads to suffering. The idea that gluttony is harmless ignores its true costs. Every act of excess diminishes something else—our capacity for generosity, time for relationships, spiritual growth, or our ability to serve others.

Gluttony isn't just about the immediate act of overconsumption; it has a ripple effect that influences every aspect of our lives. When we prioritize our desires, we often neglect the things that truly matter.

Reflecting on Our Own Gluttony

The stories shared aren't just old tales; they're a reflection of our lives today. When we fill our lives with more than we need—whether it's food, possessions, or constant busyness—we leave less room for God. I'll admit, I have way more tea than I need and more recipes than I'll ever use in a lifetime, yet I keep collecting. I often find myself lost in social media scrolling or working longer than necessary, struggling to find balance.

Where in your life might you be guilty of similar gluttony?

What are you filling your life with that keeps you distant from God?

Perhaps it's reaching for that extra serving of food, justifying it as comfort after a long day. Maybe you're pouring 'just one more' glass of wine to unwind, unaware of how it's becoming a crutch.

It might be hours lost to binge-watching Netflix or scrolling through social media, crowding out time that could be spent in prayer or quiet reflection. Alternatively, your work might consume your evenings, justified as necessary for success, yet pulling you away from your family and spiritual life.

It could also be something seemingly healthy—like exercising too much or packing your schedule with commitments—leaving no time for rest or stillness with God. These personal habits are part of a larger issue—fueled by a culture that encourages excess in every aspect of life.

The Challenge of Living in a Super-Sized World

Resisting temptation is harder than ever in today's super-sized world. The U.S. obesity rate for adults is 40.3%—tripling since 1960. As of 2023, an astonishing 73.1% are overweight or obese, making it the new normal.

Screen time has skyrocketed, with the average American spending over seven hours a day on screens in 2023. This constant digital exposure affects mental health and increases exposure to electromagnetic fields (EMFs). Online targeted advertising fuels overconsumption, encouraging impulse purchases and financial excess—evidenced by the average American credit card debt of $6,380 in the third quarter of 2023.

At the root of overconsumption is dopamine, the brain's feel-good neurotransmitter. In our super-sized world, we are constantly bombarded with stimuli designed to trigger dopamine releases, reinforcing behaviors that keep us coming back for more.

Ultra-processed foods (UPFs), carefully engineered to hit the perfect balance of sugar, salt, and fat, create a dopamine surge that drives cravings and overconsumption.

Social media platforms are built to keep us scrolling. Each like or positive comment provides a small dopamine hit, offering a fleeting sense of acceptance and validation. Over time, this constant pursuit of digital approval can become a poor substitute for genuine human connection.

Even shopping plays into this cycle. The promise of newness and self-improvement triggers dopamine, reinforcing impulsive purchases and excessive consumption.

Whether it's eating a treat, making a purchase, or receiving a social media notification, these behaviors deliver quick dopamine hits that create an addictive loop—driving overeating, overspending, and excessive screen time. Left unchecked, this cycle distances us from deeper, more lasting sources of joy.

I've felt this pull to overconsume firsthand. My husband, an enthusiastic cook, takes pride in beautiful plate presentations—but always gives me too much food. I found a simple solution: before eating, I immediately store half for lunch the next day. This one habit solved two problems—preventing overeating while giving me a ready-made meal.

As discussed above and in chapter 3, food scientists have perfected the art of engineering UPFs to hit the "bliss point," making them highly addictive. Even healthy foods can cause issues when eaten in excess, but in processed foods, excess is intentionally designed. These foods override natural fullness signals, keeping us reaching for more. What used to be three servings of soda is now considered one, and the quantity in family-sized snack packs encourages mindless overconsumption.

The push for more doesn't stop at food. Clever marketing plays on our insecurities and desires. They convince us that bigger is better, indulgence is deserved, and having endless choices equals happiness.

This super-sized mentality has permeated every aspect of modern life. Streaming services battle for our constant attention, social media never sleeps, and workplaces reward burnout over balance. We are bombarded with messages urging us to consume more, watch more, buy more.

But the impact of overconsumption goes beyond personal health. The environmental cost is staggering. The production, packaging, and disposal of endless super-sized products contribute to pollution, waste, and toxic buildup, harming not just individuals but our whole environment.

The Deception of Moderation

But what about moderation? The advice that moderation in everything is key can be misleading and even dangerous. Often used to justify indulgences, it overlooks that gluttony in any form is a sin.

I've experienced this deception firsthand. I justified my extremely long baths after work as relaxation time—sometimes even God-time or inspiration. However, more often, I spent that time reading, searching recipes, scrolling social media, or checking emails—all distractions that pulled me away from family and important work. At one point, I even became addicted to word games before deleting the app.

What I thought was moderation had become excess, stealing valuable time and connection. This taught me that moderation is often subjective—one person's moderate ice cream habit might be daily, while for another, it's three times a week. My "moderate" bath time had quietly become excessive.

Moderation is shaped by culture and history. In today's super-sized world, our moderation might once have been considered excess. Some things—like drugs or other harmful behaviors—shouldn't be done at all, even in moderation.

Biblically, moderation means being good stewards, making responsible choices, and honoring our temples. The Bible doesn't call for extreme self-denial or deprivation but for avoiding overindulgence that can lead us away from God.

The Power of Hormesis

While moderation often fails as a guiding principle, hormesis offers a better way to understand what enough really means. Hormesis involves using small, controlled stressors to make us stronger and healthier. Think of plants: they grow stronger when faced with mild challenges like wind or less water. These small stressors trigger the plants to develop ways to survive tougher conditions.

In our bodies, small stressors work similarly, causing our cells to respond and adapt. This process of hormesis activates pathways that make our bodies more resilient, better able to repair damage, and able to work at their best.

The principle of hormesis applies to many aspects of life:

- **Exercise:** Lifting weights or running builds strength and endurance, but overtraining can lead to injuries.
- **Exposure to Cold:** Brief exposure can boost immunity and improve circulation, but prolonged exposure risks damaged tissues and death.
- **Mental Challenges:** Tackling complex problems or learning new skills can improve cognitive and mental resilience, but too much mental stress can lead to anxiety, burnout, and decreased performance.
- **Dietary Restrictions:** Intermittent fasting (covered in chapter 11) or reducing certain foods can support health and reduce inflammation, but overly restrictive diets can lead to nutrient deficiencies, fatigue, and other health problems.

Understanding hormesis helps us appreciate the delicate balance our bodies require. It reminds us that while some stress can be beneficial, excess in any form—whether it's overexertion, overeating, or overindulgence in any activity—can be harmful. This concept aligns with biblical wisdom, which encourages self-control in all aspects of life.

> *But the fruit of the Spirit is love, joy, peace, patience, kindness, goodness, faithfulness, gentleness, and self-control. The law is not against such things.*
>
> (Galatians 5:22 *CSB*)

Self-Control and Hara Hachi Bu

Jesus modeled balance and intentionality, showing that our choices in food, work, and rest can honor God. Practicing self-control in these areas reflects our faith and values.

Hara Hachi Bu, the Japanese practice of eating until 80% full, promotes balance, reduces waste, and honors God by teaching us to listen to our bodies and avoid overindulgence. This practice has been especially helpful to my clients with conditions like diverticulitis, as stopping before feeling completely full reduces strain on the colon.

Hara Hachi Bu isn't about deprivation but finding satisfaction without excess. It aligns beautifully with biblical teachings on self-control. Slowing down and savoring each bite gives our bodies time to recognize fullness signals, helping to prevent overeating.

This mindset and practice help resist the world's super-sized mentality, fostering health, contentment, and a deeper spiritual connection. *Hara Hachi Bu* offers a practical way to avoid excess and honor our temples through mindful eating.

While practices like *Hara Hachi Bu* offer solutions for individuals, addressing gluttony on a broader scale requires community support. The church has a unique role in making a difference here.

The Church's Role in Addressing Gluttony

We live in a world constantly tempting us with excess. Many churches readily address various sins but often remain silent on gluttony, despite frequent biblical warnings against overindulgence. This silence may stem from its pervasiveness—a struggle shared by many, including church leaders.

As Christian philosopher Johnathon Bowers noted, "Gluttony is perhaps the most tolerated sin in American Christianity," making overindulgence feel normal within church communities.

Interestingly, research suggests that while religious or spiritual individuals tend to follow healthier diets, they also consume more food overall. Only certain religious groups—specifically the Amish, Jews, and Buddhists—consistently show lower body weights compared to the general population.

Churches have a unique opportunity to be part of the solution by openly addressing gluttony. Creating a judgment-free environment that encourages open discussion about struggles with food and excess fosters growth, support, and accountability. In this space, members can reflect on their diet, lifestyle, and spiritual lives, leading to growth in both faith and health. This openness helps us recognize how gluttony can distance us from God.

> *Therefore encourage one another and build each other up as you are already doing.*
>
> (1 Thessalonians 5:11 *CSB*)

Steps for Embracing a Balanced Life

Reflect on these questions posed earlier:

- Where am I experiencing gluttony?
- What am I filling my life with that keeps me distant from God?

Recognizing the challenges of our super-sized world is only the beginning; real change comes from taking intentional, actionable steps.

Below are some practical tips you can start implementing today:

1. **Set intentional limits and practice portion control:**

- Set small, achievable limits on triggers (e.g., social media, shopping, or advertisements).
- Use the built-in feature on your devices to alert you when you've reached a certain amount of daily screen time.
- Avoid UPFs, which can hijack your brain into wanting more.
- Use smaller plates and bowls to help manage portions, and wait about twenty minutes before going back for seconds to see if you're still hungry.
- Plan on taking leftovers home when dining out.
- Stick to regular eating schedules. Teach children (and yourself) to recognize hunger and fullness instead of eating out of boredom or habit.

2. **Cultivate gratitude and mindful eating:**

- Pause before meals or activities to thank God for His provision and seek wisdom in stewarding it well.
- Minimize distractions (e.g., TV, phones) to focus fully on your meal and enjoy the company of those eating with you.
- Slow down, savor each bite, notice the flavors and textures, and tune into your body's hunger and fullness signals.

3. Build a supportive community:

- Surround yourself with people who encourage healthy habits.
- Share your goals with a trusted friend or group for mutual accountability and check in regularly to stay on track.
- Encourage church involvement by starting discussions or joining support groups focused on balanced living from overeating or other addictions (e.g., Celebrate Recovery).
- If you're struggling to make diet or lifestyle changes on your own, consider seeking personalized advice from a qualified professional, such as a nutritionist or health coach. Look for one who specializes in mindful eating, overeating, or other eating behaviors, depending on your needs.

By implementing these steps, you can take charge of your health and well-being in a world that often promotes excess. Each small change you make can lead to a more balanced and fulfilling life, allowing you to honor both your body and your faith. Remember, it's not about perfection; it's about progress.

Lessons from a Rabbit's Wake-Up Call

Mr. Grabbit's gluttony isolated him from his community. His wake-up call came when he found himself stranded atop a church steeple. Only after the fire department rescued him did he realize the burden of his overconsumption.

Humbled by the experience, he sold his surplus possessions. He shared a meal with his neighbors and embraced a simpler, more connected way of living.

Gluttony has historically been associated with food, likely because production was labor-intensive, and items like meat, dessert, and wine were rare luxuries. But as Mr. Grabbit's story illustrates, gluttony extends beyond the table. It is a hunger for more—more food, more possessions, more distractions—often at the expense of others and in defiance of self-control.

All of a person's labor is for his stomach,
yet the appetite is never satisfied.

(Ecclesiastes 6:7 *CSB*)

We've examined how gluttony can creep into our lives, affecting our physical and spiritual well-being. From the lessons of Adam and Eve and the Israelites, we see how excess distances us from God. We've uncovered practical tools for balance in the wisdom of *Hara Hachi Bu*, hormesis, and biblical self-discipline.

So, whether you eat or drink, or whatever you do,
do everything for the glory of God.

(1 Corinthians 10:31 *CSB*)

This is our challenge: to view every choice—what we consume, how we spend our time, what we pursue—as an opportunity to honor God.

Start small. Identify one area of excess in your life and set a realistic goal for change. Invite someone to walk this journey with you. As C.S. Lewis wisely said, "Every time you make a choice you are turning the central part of you… into something a little different than it was before."

In a world constantly pushing for more, let's embrace the beauty of enough. May we find freedom in limits, joy in gratitude, and strength in community as we pursue a life that glorifies God in all things.

PART TWO

Rooted in Connections

INTRODUCTION
TO PART TWO

One Body, Many Systems

For you created my inmost being; you knit me together in my mother's womb. I praise you because I am fearfully and wonderfully made; your works are wonderful, I know that full well.

(Psalm 139:13-14 *NIV*)

It's all connected.

From the trillions of microbes in our gut to the rhythms of our daily lives, every aspect of our health is deeply intertwined. Modern medicine often treats the body as a collection of isolated parts. The truth is, our systems don't work independently from one another—they're designed to function as one integrated whole.

This integration begins in the womb, where the nervous system—one of the first systems to form—establishes the wiring that connects everything. Through the spine, it links every system—gut, heart, mind—in God's intricate design.

Chiropractic care supports these connections by aligning the spine to optimize nerve communication, working with God's design where other fields often miss the unity. While best known for outperforming medications for low back pain and easing headaches, research shows chiropractic can also:

- Improve joint health and mobility
- Reduce inflammation throughout the body
- Support digestive health through the vagus nerve
- Ease symptoms of depression and anxiety

When one system is impaired, others are impacted. Chronic inflammation, poor gut health, or oral infections ripple outward, affecting our hearts, minds, and overall well-being. This interconnectedness isn't just a challenge—it's also our greatest asset. As we address one area of imbalance, healing and vitality often spread throughout the entire body.

God designed our bodies with remarkable complexity and wisdom. Science continues to reveal how everything works together in ways we are only beginning to understand. *God's Prescription* touches on just a fraction of these connections. Each chapter could be a book on its own, but it's enough to show that we were created with intention and purpose.

In this section, we'll explore the foundational connections that sustain our health: the gut-brain-heart axis, the role of inflammation in tying everything together, the surprising links between oral health and chronic disease, and the strength of our bones as they reflect the strength of our bodies. These systems aren't just physical; they influence our emotions, our energy, and even our spiritual clarity.

Understanding how "it's all connected" empowers us to make meaningful changes—ones that support the health of our whole selves, not just our individual parts. By nurturing these foundational systems, we align ourselves with how we were designed to thrive.

CHAPTER 5

The Unbreakable Connection Between Mind, Body, and Spirit

Now may the God of peace Himself sanctify you completely.
And may your whole spirit, soul, and body be kept sound and
blameless at the coming of our Lord Jesus Christ.

(1 Thessalonians 5:23 *CSB*)

One day, when my four-year-old grandson went home from our house, he delivered a piece of wisdom so profound it caught his mother off guard. "Mom, you shouldn't get angry at me. It makes unhealthy chemicals in your body." His mother laughed, advising him that wasn't going to get him out of trouble. But where had he heard that? Had he unknowingly stumbled onto a truth far deeper than he realized?

Our thoughts, beliefs, emotions, and faith can literally change our health at the cellular level, and science continues to affirm what Scripture has been teaching us all along:

A cheerful heart is good medicine,
but a crushed spirit dries up the bones.

(Proverbs 17:22 *NIV*)

Paul's final greeting in 1 Thessalonians 5:23 isn't just a wish—it's a blueprint for wholeness. Our mind, body, and spirit are not separate, independent parts of who we are. They're intricately woven together, designed by God to work in harmony and constantly influencing one another.

True well-being is built on a foundation of thoughts shaped by truth and hope, beliefs anchored in God's promises, emotions grounded in gratitude and peace, and a clear sense of meaning and purpose. As you read this chapter, think of how you can align your thoughts, emotions, and actions with God's design for wholeness and peace.

Mindset—The Lens Through Which We See the World

"Change the way you look at things,
and the things you look at will change."

—Wayne Dyer

Mindset isn't just *what* we think—it's *how* we think. It's the patterns of thought, core beliefs, and assumptions we carry about ourselves, others, and life itself. Whether we approach life with hope or fear, optimism or cynicism—these mental patterns become the lens through which we interpret reality. They influence how we respond to opportunities and challenges.

Our thoughts shape our emotional responses, which in turn drive our behaviors. Over time, these behaviors form habits, ultimately impacting our overall health and well-being—positively or negatively.

The brain perceives the world, interprets it, and sends biochemical messages to every cell in the body, dictating whether they are in growth, repair, or defense mode—even affecting how genes are expressed. Through epigenetics, we know our genes aren't rigid blueprints; their expression is influenced by our mental and emotional states.

The Mind-Body Connection

Mind-body medicine, once dismissed as pseudoscience or "woo-woo," is now solidly backed by research showing how thoughts and beliefs create physiological realities. This chapter focuses on the profound connection between mind, body, and spirit. Consider these research-backed examples of the mind-body connection:

- **Inflammation:** Research shows that a positive mindset and optimism reduce inflammatory markers like C-reactive protein (CRP) and interleukin-6 (IL-6).

- **Oxidative Stress:** Present-focused practices have been shown to reduce oxidative stress, protecting cells from damage.

- **Immune Function:** Mind-body practices and a positive mindset are associated with enhanced immune function, including increased natural killer (NK) cell activity, which helps defend against infections and disease.

- **Longevity and Disease Prevention:** A positive mindset is associated with better overall health, fewer illnesses, and increased longevity.

- **Hormones:** Those with a positive, empowered mindset have lower cortisol levels and more balanced hormones. Research shows that power poses—expansive, open stances—can help shift mindset and hormone levels. For more on power poses, see the Resources.

- **Gene Expression:** Research shows that relaxation and meditation techniques can downregulate genes associated with stress responses and upregulate those linked to immune resilience.

- **Generational Health:** Research suggests the placenta acts as a "third brain," transmitting a mother's physiological state to her baby, potentially affecting health across generations.

These aren't abstract findings—they show up in real lives, every day in measurable ways.

The good news is that our mindset isn't fixed; it can be intentionally reshaped. With awareness, practice, and consistency, we can learn to redirect our thoughts, challenge unhelpful beliefs, and cultivate patterns that support our health and well-being.

Managing Emotions and Building Resistance

In a world where connection is at our fingertips, we find ourselves more isolated than ever. Loneliness is more dangerous to our health and longevity than obesity or smoking. As our social bonds fray, so too does our mental well-being. The most recent CDC data shows that 17.7% of women, 8.4% of men, and nearly one in four women aged 60 or older use antidepressants. These statistics paint a sobering picture of our collective emotional state.

Emotional health affects much more than just our mood. Fear, stress, and unresolved trauma cause physical changes in the body, impacting every system and draining our ability to thrive. Research shows that negative emotions, especially suppressed anger or a hostile outlook, can greatly raise the risk of illness and even early death.

Fear and Stress: The Silent Thieves of Health

Two powerful forces often used by the enemy to attack our peace and health are fear and stress. Both trigger similar responses in the body, known as the fight-or-flight response. This reaction is managed by the emotional (or limbic) brain, bypassing logical thought. In this state, heart rate, blood pressure, and breathing increase as the adrenal glands release stress hormones like adrenaline and cortisol. Essential functions like digestion, detoxification, and deep cellular repair are put on hold.

In severe cases, the fight-or-flight response can trigger panic attacks—sudden episodes of intense fear paired with strong physical symptoms. These attacks vividly show how our thoughts and emotions can instantly and powerfully affect our bodies.

While this reaction can protect us in short bursts by helping us react quickly to danger, chronic activation keeps our bodies in a state of high alert. Over time, chronic activation drains our energy, exhausts our minds, disrupts sleep, and contributes to inflammation, weight gain, and even disease.

Persistent fear and stress can influence the progression of:

- Cardiovascular disease
- Autoimmune disorders
- Gastrointestinal disorders
- Cancer
- Diabetes
- Epilepsy
- Parkinson's
- Osteoporosis
- Accelerated aging
- Infertility
- Depression and anxiety

Stress can lead to unhealthy habits like teeth-grinding, smoking, and drinking. It contributes to the majority of primary care visits, and around one million people miss work each day because of it. Most importantly, stress and fear rob us of joy and connection with God and others.

Scripture offers a path to peace:

Do not be anxious about anything, but in every situation, by prayer and petition, with thanksgiving, present your requests to God. And the peace of God, which transcends all understanding, will guard your hearts and your minds in Christ Jesus.

(Philippians 4:6-7 *NIV*)

Scripture doesn't call us to pretend everything is fine. Instead, it instructs us to align our thoughts with truth, hope, and faith, even in the face of difficulty. Acknowledging the impact of fear and stress is the first step toward reclaiming our peace.

Healing Emotional Wounds

Sometimes, fear and stress have deep roots. Trauma—whether from a single event or prolonged experiences—doesn't just linger in our memories; it leaves an imprint on our bodies and minds. As Dr. Bessel van der Kolk explains in *The Body Keeps the Score*, trauma can rewire the brain, dysregulate the nervous system, and trap us in cycles of hypervigilance and chronic fear.

Anxiety and depression often arise from imbalances in the mind, body, and spirit. Anxiety keeps our focus on future fears, while depression anchors us in past regrets—both robbing us of the present moment. While medical treatment may be needed, true healing also requires addressing root causes, such as chronic stress, poor nutrition, and spiritual disconnection.

Cast all your anxiety on him because he cares for you.

(1 Peter 5:7 *NIV*)

Sometimes, the weight of emotional burdens is too heavy to carry alone, and professional help may be necessary. Seeking support isn't weakness, it's wise stewardship of the bodies and minds God has entrusted to us.

Plans fail for lack of counsel, but with
many advisers they succeed.

(Proverbs 15:22 *NIV*)

Gratitude and forgiveness are powerful tools for healing (1 Thessalonians 5:18; Luke 6:37). Research shows gratitude lowers blood pressure, improves sleep, and strengthens emotional resilience. Similarly, forgiveness eases emotional burdens, reduces stress, and supports healing. These aren't just feel-good ideas—they're proven strategies for mental, emotional, and physical health.

True healing isn't about eliminating every negative thought or emotion. It's about building resilience, deepening our relationship with God, and trusting Him with what we can't control. When we combine faith with intentional action, we step into the wholeness God desires for us.

The Power of Belief

"Whether you think you can, or you
think you can't—you're right."

—Henry Ford

Our beliefs aren't just a collection of thoughts. They're what we accept as truth and allow to shape our actions. For example, if we believe a situation is hopeless, we will act (or fail to act) accordingly.

Doctors might say, "There's nothing more we can do." But Scripture tells us, *"For nothing will be impossible with God."* (Luke 1:37 *CSB*).

When we resign ourselves to a diagnosis, condition, or circumstance without seeking God's wisdom or believing in His power to intervene, we aren't just giving up on our health—we're disconnecting from the hope Christ offers.

Belief and Healing

Research shows that belief, whether positive or negative, can greatly impact health and healing. For example:

- A *Lancet* study found that patients who believed their treatment would work had better outcomes, even when receiving a placebo. In contrast, the Framingham Heart Study revealed that women who believed they were prone to heart disease were nearly four times more likely to die from it, regardless of their actual risk factors.

- Another study revealed that practitioners' belief in a patient's ability to heal played a significant role in recovery rates. When a doctor or therapist conveyed genuine belief in their patient's potential for healing, the patient's body often responded more positively to treatment.

This effect isn't just psychological; it's physiological. Belief can lower cortisol, enhance the immune response, and trigger the release of endorphins and dopamine, which aid healing and reduce pain. Whether through faith, trust in a treatment, or confidence in a practitioner, believing in the possibility of healing activates powerful physiological responses.

The Placebo and Nocebo Effects

The placebo effect, sometimes called remembered wellness, occurs when the body recalls a state of health, triggering natural healing mechanisms. In contrast, the nocebo effect shows the harm negative expectations can cause. Patients expecting treatment failure or side effects are more likely to experience them.

This reveals a profound truth: Your body listens to your beliefs.

The Science of Faith

Modern science confirms what Scripture has long taught: faith and belief directly affect physical health outcomes. While mindset focuses on how we think, faith taps into what we believe about God, our purpose, and our future. It's not just a mental or emotional state—it's a transformative force that impacts our physical well-being.

Research shows that faith-based practices like prayer, gratitude, and forgiveness aren't just spiritual disciplines; they can physically change the brain and body, lower stress hormones, improve immune function, facilitate coping, and promote healing.

Literature reviews of numerous studies show religious involvement is associated with better health outcomes. The findings are striking:

- **Lower Risk of Mortality:** Regular attendance of religious services was associated with a 37% greater likelihood of living longer compared to non-attendees or less frequent attendees.
- **Better Mental Health:** Religion and spirituality have been linked to lower levels of depression, anxiety, and suicide along with greater emotional resilience.
- **Stronger Immune Function:** Religious involvement has been shown to lower infection rates and viral loads.
- **Better Cardiovascular Health:** Religious participation is associated with lower blood pressure and a reduced risk of cardiovascular disease.

Faith isn't just a spiritual comfort. It's a biological advantage. Harold Koenig, MD, a leading researcher in faith and health outcomes, summarizes it well, "Faith doesn't make life easier, but it does make it more manageable. It provides hope, meaning, and a sense of purpose, which directly impact health outcomes."

Faith and Healing: The Spiritual Connection

By his wounds, you have been healed.

(1 Peter 2:24 *CSB*)

Did you know that healing is part of God's redemption plan? It isn't earned; it's received by faith when we accept Jesus. His sacrifice didn't just secure our salvation; it purchased our healing. That's why healing and forgiveness often appear together in Scripture (Psalm 103:3, John 5:14, Luke 5:20-24, James 5:15-16).

Sickness—whether physical, emotional, or spiritual—often finds its roots in sin. It may not be personal wrongdoing, but sin's presence in our fallen world. Emotions like unforgiveness, guilt, shame, and condemnation can disrupt our well-being, keeping us bound in cycles of brokenness.

A thief comes only to steal and kill and destroy. I have come so that they may have life and have it in abundance.

(John 10:10 *CSB*)

Correcting Misguided Beliefs

One of the enemy's greatest tactics is distorting God's promises. Misunderstanding Scripture keeps people trapped in sickness and doubt. These misconceptions are sometimes reinforced by tradition or cultural teaching, and until I closely studied God's Word, I believed many of them. So, let's examine each belief and what Scripture actually says:

1. **God heals selectively:** The idea that God heals some but not others contradicts His nature. He doesn't forgive selectively, and Jesus didn't die for some. His sacrifice was for all. *"He did not even spare his own Son, but gave him up for us all. How will he not also with Him, grant us everything?"* (Romans 8:32 *CSB*).

2. **Divine healing no longer occurs:** Healing didn't stop with the apostles. Scripture never suggests an expiration date on God's promises. *"And these signs will accompany those who believe: In my name... they will lay hands on the sick, and they will get well"* (Mark 16:17-18 CSB).

3. **Sickness is sometimes God's will:** God using sickness to teach, humble, or discipline us is not Scriptural. Paul's thorn (2 Corinthians 12:7-10) wasn't a physical illness but a source of persecution—a messenger from Satan. Paul's telling Timothy to drink a little wine for his stomach issues (1 Timothy 5:23) wasn't evidence of withheld healing. It was wisdom and practical advice for an issue likely caused by unclean water. Job's suffering wasn't God's desire; it was Satan's attack (Job 2:7).

4. **Jesus didn't heal everyone:** Divine healing requires both believing and receiving. Jesus healed all who came to Him in faith (Matthew 8:16), but in places where unbelief was strong, His ability to perform miracles was limited (Mark 6:5-6).

Not everyone receives healing, but that doesn't mean healing wasn't available or that God's promises failed. It's easy to fall into the trap of blaming God or trying to explain someone else's experience. But as Jesus said to Peter, *"What is that to you? As for you, follow me"* (John 21:22 CSB). Another person's unanswered prayer doesn't diminish God's ability or willingness to answer yours.

It's not enough to believe in God or salvation; we must also believe God's Word on healing. Jesus frequently told those He healed that their faith had made them well (Mark 5:34, Mark 10:52, Luke 17:17-19). We must declare God's promises and align our mindset with His truth. Those who lay hands on us or pray for us should also believe in divine healing, and we should surround ourselves with believers.

While God can and does work through medical care, only He offers true healing and is all knowing. Pray for God to guide your practitioners, but don't let their care replace faith.

Healing miracles are still happening today. For a deeper exploration of biblical healing principles and real-life healing testimonies, I recommend *Healing Basics* by Pastor Mark Boer.

Living with Purpose and Intention

> *For we are God's handiwork, created in Christ Jesus to do good works, which God prepared in advance for us to do.*

(Ephesians 2:10 *NIV*)

God's desire isn't just for us to survive. He wants us to thrive and fulfill the purpose He's given us. Living in health and wholeness equips us to fulfill our calling, but poor health can rob us of the energy, focus, and clarity required.

Research shows that people with a strong sense of purpose experience better health, greater resilience, and even longer lifespans. In *Man's Search for Meaning*, Viktor Frankl observed that survivors of the Holocaust often shared one common trait: an unwavering sense of purpose. He wrote, "Those who have a 'why' to live can bear almost any 'how.'"

When we align our mindset with God's purpose, our health becomes a tool to fulfill His plan for our lives.

Faith in Action: Stewarding Your Health Journey

> *For just as the body without the spirit is dead, so also faith without works is dead.*

(James 2:26 *CSB*)

Our thoughts, beliefs, and choices are not isolated; they ripple outward, impacting our health, our families, our communities, and even the legacy we leave behind. This impact requires intentionality and active stewardship over what God has entrusted to us.

It's easy to fall into patterns of blame—whether on genetics, circumstances, fate, or even God. But science confirms what Scripture teaches: our choices, beliefs, and mindset deeply affect our health outcomes.

> "Insight + Action = Results. Insight – Action = Regret."
>
> —Amber Setter, PCC

True insight comes from *knowing* the truth (John 8:32). When we act on God's truth, we step into the freedom and healing He offers. The Holy Spirit is our helper, but the work is ours to do. Aligning our actions with our faith allows us to honor God, care for our bodies, and positively influence those around us.

Practical Steps for Healing

You don't need the perfect moment, a mountain retreat, or hours of meditation to reset your mind. Sometimes, all it takes is one pause, one deep breath, and one prayer. Chapter 11 goes deeper into mindfulness practices and relaxation techniques, but you can begin calming your mind, reducing cortisol, and aligning your mind, body, and spirit right now.

These intentional steps can help align your body, mind, and spirit with God's healing promises:

- **Gratitude Journaling:** Each evening, write three things you're thankful for to reduce stress and anchor yourself in the present.
- **Healing Scriptures Recording:** Record yourself reading healing Scriptures aloud and listen daily. Hearing God's Word activates faith and reinforces His promises.

- **Anointing with Oil:** Use oil as a physical symbol of God's healing power (James 5:14-15). Essential oils like frankincense offer anti-inflammatory and stress-relieving benefits.

- **Forgiveness Practice:** Release resentment toward others and yourself. Forgiveness doesn't excuse harm or require reconciliation; it's a process of surrendering hurt to God, day by day, and praying for the person involved.

- **Laughter Therapy:** Watch a funny movie, spend time with someone who makes you laugh, or intentionally seek joy. Laughter releases endorphins, reduces stress hormones, and promotes healing.

This isn't an exhaustive list, but it's a good starting point. Healing begins with one step—one choice to believe followed by one act of faith.

Wisdom Beyond His Years

As we conclude this chapter on the unbreakable connection between mind, body, and spirit, let's return to my grandson's story and see how a simple insight from a child unveils a profound truth.

After that evening when my grandson told his mother not to get angry, my son asked me, "Did you tell your grandson that getting angry makes unhealthy chemicals in your body?" I smiled and said, "Yes, I explained to him how our emotions can affect our health." In his innocent brilliance, he had taken that truth and repurposed it.

Isn't that just like God to use the innocence of a child to remind us of something so profound?

Our emotions and thoughts have real, physical effects on our bodies. Just as anger can create "unhealthy chemicals," choosing positive thoughts and emotions, exercising faith, and aligning with God's Word can create "healthy chemicals" that promote healing and well-being. This isn't just a nice idea—it's part of God's redemptive plan for us.

The question isn't whether healing is available. The question is: Will you receive it?

CHAPTER 6

Every Part Matters:
The Gut-Brain-Heart Connection

"All disease begins in the gut."

—Hippocrates

Decades ago, I would joke that I couldn't stray far from a bathroom, but it really wasn't funny. Every morning felt like my gut held me hostage. Pain, bloating, and relentless trips to the toilet were just the start. Then came sleepless nights, fatigue, brain fog, and body pain that clung to me like a wet blanket.

The struggle consumed my life, keeping me from giving my best to my family and work. I'd wake not wanting to move or get up. At night, I struggled to sleep through the pain, wondering if tomorrow would be better or worse.

Doctors gave me bucket diagnoses (labels for symptoms) without identifying a root cause. First, it was irritable bowel syndrome (IBS). Then, when things didn't improve, fibromyalgia. They offered no solutions, only pain relievers, sleep aids, and recommendations to exercise.

I didn't want to rely on pills forever, and exercising often made things worse. I felt desperate. I tried Zoloft and Ambien. Zoloft flatlined my emotions, and while on Ambien, I had two minor car accidents—something research shows isn't uncommon. I also experimented with diet and supplements, yet nothing touched the root problem. My gut was screaming for help, but no one seemed to hear me—not the doctors, not even my husband, who was almost as frustrated as I was.

Deep down, I knew there was a root cause. My symptoms weren't random; they had to be connected. Since it all started in my gut, that's where I began my mission to reclaim my health naturally.

The Gut: Where Health Begins

Around 400 BC, the father of medicine, Hippocrates, was one of the first to abandon magic and superstition in his practice. Instead, he used observation and logic. He couldn't have known about the gut's trillions of microbes or its role in immune function, yet he recognized a clear connection between disease and poor gut health.

While his statement, "All disease begins in the gut," may not apply universally, it holds true more often than not. The gut is foundational to our physical, metabolic, immune, and emotional health.

In functional medicine, gut health is emphasized, and whether I'm working with a client with an autoimmune disease or a skin disease, I always start in the gut.

> *"When you don't know where to start, you can make a lot of progress by starting with the gut."*
>
> —Mark Hyman, MD

Your Amazing Digestive System

To understand gut health, let's take a quick tour of your gastrointestinal (GI) tract.

Your gut isn't just your stomach; it's the entire GI tract, stretching from mouth to anus, connecting your body to the outside world. This complex system is a finely tuned orchestra, with each step relying on the previous one. It involves multiple organs working in perfect harmony to extract nutrients, defend against pathogens, and eliminate waste.

Digestion actually begins in the brain. The sight, smell, or thought of food triggers saliva production, preparing your mouth to break food down both chemically with enzymes and mechanically with chewing. So, when you were told as a child to chew thoroughly, you were actually being taught the first step of proper digestion.

As you swallow food, the esophagus muscles move it to your stomach. Once there, stomach acid and enzymes continue breaking it down while neutralizing harmful pathogens that hitch a ride. Low stomach acid or acid-suppressing medication can disrupt this step, affecting downstream nutrient breakdown, enzyme activation, and bile release, leaving you vulnerable to poor digestion and nutrient deficiencies.

Next stop: the small intestine—a 21-foot-long powerhouse. Here, fat and acidity from your food signal the release of mucus and hormones. Your gallbladder releases bile to break down fats, while your pancreas releases enzymes that break down proteins, fats, and carbohydrates. As food moves through, nutrients enter your bloodstream through the intestinal lining. If this lining becomes damaged or "leaky," undigested food particles, bacteria, and toxins can slip into your bloodstream. Your immune system sees these as threats and launches a defense, which triggers inflammation throughout your body.

From there, nutrients travel to your liver, which processes these nutrients, detoxifies harmful substances, and distributes building blocks throughout your body.

The final stop before exiting your body is the large intestine (colon), where gut bacteria break down fiber, produce vitamins, and create short-chain fatty acids (SCFAs).

As you can see, each step in this process relies on the one before it. When one falters, the entire system is impacted.

Digestion isn't the gut's only job. Inside this complex system, biochemical communication happens constantly, influencing your mood, sleep, focus, and emotional resilience. This communication starts with neurotransmitters—chemical messengers your body produces using key nutrients from your food.

Gut Health and Neurotransmitters

Imagine eating a protein-rich meal of turkey or eggs, both good sources of tryptophan (an essential amino acid). However, if your body lacks sufficient stomach acid to properly break down protein into amino acids, it can't fully access these vital building blocks. Each amino acid plays an important role, and tryptophan, in particular, is key for producing serotonin.

Serotonin is a neurotransmitter that helps regulate mood and relaxation. It is also used to produce melatonin, the hormone that regulates your sleep-wake cycle, supports your immune system, and helps repair cells while promoting healthy aging.

Neurotransmitters (e.g., serotonin and dopamine) are primarily manufactured during deep sleep, so without enough quality sleep, metabolic disruption occurs. Research shows this can increase the risk of cardiovascular events and death from all causes. Remarkably, about 95% of your serotonin and around 50% of your dopamine are produced in your gut. However, if your gut isn't functioning well, serotonin production can plummet, and dopamine signaling may be disrupted.

This creates a vicious cycle, leading to a cascade of issues: anxiety, depression, poor sleep due to low melatonin levels, reduced motivation, and a lack of focus.

When patients see conventional doctors for symptoms like anxiety, low mood, irritability, fatigue, poor sleep, brain fog, muscle pain, or digestive issues, they're often given an SSRI (selective serotonin reuptake inhibitor) like Paxil or Zoloft. But here's the catch: SSRIs don't make your body produce more serotonin; they just help the existing serotonin stay in your system longer. For ongoing sleep problems, doctors might also prescribe sleep aids, as I experienced during my struggle with fibromyalgia.

What if there was a better way?

What if targeted diet and lifestyle changes could address the root cause of this imbalance? No one has an SSRI deficiency, but nutritional deficiencies are common and often overlooked.

The Enteric Nervous System: Our Second Brain

Your gut's influence on your brain doesn't stop with chemical messengers like serotonin and melatonin. It also relies on a network of nerves called the Enteric Nervous System (ENS) that is so sophisticated researchers like Dr. Michael Gershon have referred to the gut as our "second brain." The ENS has far more nerve cells than in your spinal cord.

The ENS helps control:

- **Digestion** – by coordinating the movement of food through your gut, regulating enzyme secretion, and managing nutrient absorption.
- **Immune responses** – by interacting with immune cells to detect and respond to threats in your gut.
- **Inflammation** – by regulating inflammatory processes through enteric glial cells.
- **Gut hormone release** – by influencing the secretion of hormones that regulate digestion and the feeling of fullness (satiety).
- **Local blood flow** – by adjusting blood flow to different parts of your digestive system as needed.

The ENS maintains constant communication with your central nervous system through the vagus nerve and other signaling pathways.

The Bible Knew It First

In ancient Hebrew and Greek cultures, emotions were often described as residing in the "bowels" (me'eh in Hebrew and splagchnon in Greek). These terms referred literally to the intestines but were metaphorically used to express deep emotional experiences—compassion, sorrow, and even love.

My bowels, my bowels! I am pained at my very heart.

(Jeremiah 4:19 *KJV*)

For God is my record, how greatly I long after you all in the bowels of Jesus Christ.

(Philippians 1:8 *KJV*)

While modern translations often replace "bowels" with "heart" or "mind," the ancient metaphor captures a truth that science now validates: the gut isn't just a digestive organ—it's deeply connected to our emotional and mental health.

Today, we know the gut produces neurotransmitters, communicates through the vagus nerve, and reacts strongly to emotional states. It seems the ancient writers were onto something: nurturing gut health isn't just about digestion; it's also essential for emotional and mental well-being.

The Vagus Nerve: The Gut-Brain Superhighway

If the ENS is your second brain, the vagus nerve is the superhighway connecting it to your first brain. This long nerve stretches from your brainstem to your gut, lungs, heart, and other organs, allowing information to travel both ways.

When functioning properly, the vagus nerve helps:

- **Regulate digestion:** It signals the stomach to make acid, the pancreas to release digestive enzymes, the gallbladder to release bile, and the intestines to move food along.
- **Reduce inflammation:** It calms immune responses and prevents tissue damage from excess inflammation.
- **Maintain gut barrier function:** It supports a strong gut lining, preventing undesirable substances from passing into your bloodstream.
- **Support mental health:** It influences mood regulation and stress resilience.
- **Calm the body:** It acts like a gear shift, transitioning your body from a sympathetic (fight-or-flight) state to a parasympathetic (rest-and-digest) healing state.
- **Signal fullness:** It communicates satiety signals to the brain after eating.

When vagal tone is poor, these functions can break down, leading to chronic inflammation and poor gut-brain communication. Over time, this can cause a range of emotional and physical health problems.

Factors that can disrupt vagal tone (a measure of vagus nerve function) include:

- Stress
- Poor diet (e.g., ultra-processed foods and unhealthy fats)
- Lack of physical activity
- Chronic inflammation
- Cervical spine issues (e.g., nerve compression)
- Sleep disturbances

Research links poor vagal tone to conditions such as leaky gut, depression, post-traumatic stress disorder (PTSD), cardiovascular diseases, inflammatory bowel disease, IBS, autoimmune disorders, and epilepsy. Studies also show that shortly after a traumatic brain injury, both the blood-brain barrier and the gut barrier can become disrupted, highlighting the deep interconnection of these systems.

Your gut's influence extends beyond digestion, affecting mood, sleep, and emotional resilience. It also communicates with your brain and heart, forming a powerful three-way connection. While much remains to be discovered and understood, one thing is clear: supporting your vagus nerve is essential for a healthy gut-brain connection. Techniques like relaxation, deep breathing, and mindfulness can improve vagal tone, enhance resilience, and restore balance between your gut and brain.

The Gut-Brain-Heart Connection

The vagus nerve serves as a communication link between the gut, brain, and heart, influencing heart rate, blood pressure, inflammation, and stress responses. After periods of stress or perceived danger, the vagus nerve helps shift your body out of the sympathetic state. It slows your heart rate, lowers blood pressure, and reduces cortisol release. This transition promotes relaxation, recovery, and healing.

Key heart-gut connections through the vagus nerve include:

- **Heart Rate Variability (HRV):** A measure of vagal tone, HRV reflects your body's ability to adapt to stress by measuring the variation in time between heartbeats. Higher HRV often indicates better nervous system balance, heart health, and stress resilience. (See Action Steps for ways to measure and improve HRV.)

- **Inflammation Control:** Vagus nerve stimulation can reduce inflammatory cytokines, protecting both the heart and gut lining from damage caused by chronic inflammation.
- **Stress Response:** A properly functioning vagus nerve helps lessen the long-term effects of chronic stress on the cardiovascular and digestive systems.

While the vagus nerve acts as a superhighway of communication, the real drivers of gut health are the trillions of microbes living within you. These microscopic residents influence everything from digestion and inflammation to mood and immune function.

Let's take a closer look at the gut microbiome—a world within you that can either be your greatest ally or your worst enemy.

The Microbiome: Friend or Foe?

Your gut houses a vast ecosystem of trillions of microorganisms—bacteria, fungi, viruses, and archaea—collectively known as the microbiome. While scientists once believed that bacteria outnumber human cells by a ratio of 10:1, we now know it's closer to 1:1. Compared to our ancestors, we've lost a significant number of bacterial species, at least in part due to modern lifestyles, reducing overall microbial diversity.

Our understanding of the microbiome is still in the early stages with much to be discovered. This section offers a glimpse into its profound influence on health.

In most cases, this microbial community exists in harmony with us in a symbiotic relationship: we provide microbes with food and shelter, and in return, they aid in digestion, produce vital nutrients, regulate our immune system, and even influence our mood and behavior.

Microbial balance is key. When beneficial microbes thrive, they act as powerful protectors of our health. Conversely, when this ecosystem falls out of balance—a state known as dysbiosis—these same microbes can become harmful. Dysbiosis is marked by a loss of beneficial strains, an overgrowth of harmful microbes, or reduced microbial diversity.

For most conditions I research and write about, dysbiosis plays a role in their development. This imbalance can trigger inflammation and contribute to various disorders. It has been linked to obesity, autoimmune diseases, metabolic diseases, mental health disorders, and chronic inflammation.

Microbial Balance Disruptors

Factors that can disrupt microbial balance include:

- Cesarean birth
- Infant formula feeding
- Antibiotic use
- Soil sterilization (modern agriculture)
- High-sugar, low-fiber diets
- Environmental toxins (e.g., pesticides, heavy metals)
- Excessive alcohol consumption
- Chronic stress
- Poor sleep quality

Understanding what disrupts microbial balance helps us appreciate the vital roles gut microbes play in our health.

The Many Roles of Gut Microbes

Your microbiota aren't just passive passengers; they play active roles in nearly every aspect of your health, including:

- **Nutrient Production and Absorption:** Gut bacteria produce SCFAs like butyrate, which reduce inflammation, fuel intestinal cells, and protect the gut lining. They also make vitamins K, B1, B2, and B12.

- **Central Nervous System (CNS) Communication:** Gut microbes communicate with the CNS through pathways involving the vagus nerve, immune system, microbial metabolites like SCFAs, and neurotransmitters.

- **Immune System Training:** 70 to 80% of your immune system resides in your gut, where microbes help train immune cells to respond appropriately to threats.

- **Weight Regulation:** Certain bacterial strains can influence metabolism, appetite, and fat storage.

- **Inflammation Control:** Healthy gut bacteria regulate inflammatory pathways, influencing systemic inflammation.

Gut Microbes and Mental Health

The gut-brain axis extends to the microbiome, where certain bacterial strains, often referred to as psychobiotics, can influence mental health. Studies show that probiotics can:

- Reduce anxiety-like behaviors.
- Improve cognition and concentration.
- Reduce psychological distress.
- Enhance mood and emotional resilience.

Research highlights that probiotic effects are strain-specific, not species-specific. For example, *Bifidobacterium longum* 35624 has been shown to improve anxiety and depression. However, these benefits may not apply to other strains of *Bifidobacterium longum*. Simply recommending "probiotics" is as nonspecific as a doctor prescribing "medication" without specifying the drug name or dosage.

Test, Don't Guess

Your microbiome is as unique as your fingerprint, and making uninformed changes can backfire. The wrong probiotics or diet choices might feed harmful bacteria instead of helpful ones. Stool testing can give you a clearer picture of your gut's bacterial balance, any harmful overgrowths, and how well your microbiome is producing SCFAs and other key compounds.

When the Fortress Falls: Understanding Leaky Gut

Stomach acid is the body's first line of defense against ingested pathogens, but the intestinal lining provides an additional barrier, preventing harmful substances from entering the bloodstream.

This barrier, just a single layer of cells thick, isn't foolproof. When damaged, bacteria, toxins, undigested food particles, and allergens can pass through—a condition known as leaky gut. Once dismissed by many doctors, it's now recognized as *intestinal permeability*, backed by research and diagnosable through testing.

When these substances enter the bloodstream, the immune system perceives them as threats, triggering inflammation that can contribute to autoimmune disease and other chronic health issues.

Factors known to increase gut permeability include:

- Chronic inflammation
- Poor diet (gluten, processed foods, emulsifiers, fructose, unhealthy fats, low fiber)
- Food intolerances/sensitivities
- Stress
- Genetic predisposition
- Intense exercise (Moderate exercise supports gut health.)
- Alcohol consumption
- Tobacco smoke
- Dysbiosis (gut microbial imbalance)
- Nutrient deficiencies (e.g., vitamins A, D, E, C, B vitamins, SCFAs)
- Certain medications (e.g., nonsteroidal anti-inflammatory drugs or NSAIDs, antibiotics, corticosteroids, birth control pills, acid-reducing medications)
- Environmental toxins

Protecting and restoring this barrier is key to reducing inflammation, preventing autoimmunity, and addressing the root cause of many diseases.

The 5Rs of Functional Medicine for Gut Healing

Conventional medicine often overlooks the connection between gut health, metabolism, and physical or mental disorders. Functional medicine, however, takes a whole-body approach, focusing on root causes. It recognizes that symptoms like anxiety, depression, and inflammation often stem from poor gut and metabolic health.

By addressing gut health, overall health can improve, including brain and heart function. Functional medicine evaluates diet, sleep, stress, exercise, and other lifestyle factors, using the 5Rs as a structured path to healing. While these steps provide a framework, they should be tailored to each individual's needs under the guidance of a functional medicine practitioner.

Here's how the 5Rs might look in gut healing:

1. **Remove:** Identify and eliminate factors disrupting gut health, including harmful bacteria, yeast, or parasites. Use an elimination diet or food sensitivity testing to identify trigger foods.

2. **Replace:** Support digestion with enzymes, hydrochloric acid, and bile acids, as needed. Address nutrient deficiencies like B vitamins, zinc, and magnesium, ideally informed by nutrient testing.

3. **Reinoculate:** Restore microbial balance with strain-specific probiotics tailored to your imbalances, prebiotic foods (e.g., garlic, onions, asparagus), and fermented foods (e.g., raw sauerkraut, kimchi, kefir). Probiotics that show protective effects on the intestinal barrier include *Lactobacillus rhamnosus* GG, *E. coli* Nissle 1917 and *Bifidobacterium animalis* subsp. *lactis* BB-12.

4. **Repair:** Heal the gut lining with nutrients like L-glutamine, zinc carnosine, collagen peptides, and quercetin.

5. **Rebalance:** Manage stress with prayer, gratitude, or Scripture meditation. Prioritize sleep, exercise regularly, and eat a nutrient-dense, anti-inflammatory diet.

Oh, how I wish I had the 5R framework and guidance of a functional medicine practitioner during my healing journey. I'm grateful to be on the other side of the pain I once endured, but my path was longer and harder than necessary.

The turning point came through my granddaughter's pain. As an infant, she cried in agony if her mom ate gluten before breastfeeding. Then, my adult son admitted to struggling with bloating, especially after drinking beer.

Testing revealed that celiac disease runs in our family. Eliminating gluten completely allowed my body to heal deeply for the first time. The improvement was so profound that I refuse to reintroduce gluten—not even for testing.

That healing changed everything, igniting my passion for the work I do today. I want the freedom, vitality, and joy I now experience for everyone.

Overcoming Challenges and Action Steps

Healing can start simply with one small step. Choose one action step to focus on this week, and remember that consistency, not perfection, is key.

1. **Start a Food Journal:** Track what you eat and how you feel afterward to uncover diet-symptom connections.

2. **Eat One Fermented Food Daily:** Introduce beneficial bacteria with raw sauerkraut, fermented pickles, kimchi, kefir, or yogurt without added sugar.

3. **Track Your Heart Rate Variability (HRV):** If you have access to a wearable device, monitor your HRV daily for a week. Higher HRV often indicates better vagal tone, stress resilience, and nervous system balance. Don't stress about daily numbers. Focus on trends and building habits that improve HRV.

4. **Support Vagal Tone:** Choose one new daily practice to do for at least 10 minutes: breathwork, singing, gargling, Scripture meditation, or listening to music designed to stimulate the vagus nerve (e.g., binaural beats or relaxation tracks).

5. **Massage Your Vagus Nerve:** Stimulate your vagus nerve by gently massaging the area behind your earlobes with clove and lime essential oils.

6. **Consider Chiropractic:** Regular adjustments can support the body's ability to shift to a parasympathetic state, enhance HRV, and improve vagal tone.

Every Part Matters

Just as a body, though one, has many parts, but all its many parts form one body, so it is with Christ.

(1 Corinthians 12:12 *NIV*)

The Bible tells us that every part of the body is valuable and serves a purpose. Modern science echoes this truth, revealing that even the so-called "unimportant" organs, like the appendix and gallbladder, play important roles in our health.

Your gut, brain, heart, and immune system are not isolated parts—they are interconnected, interdependent, and constantly communicating. True healing starts from within, and by healing your gut, you're also reclaiming your life.

"Learn how to see. Realize that everything connects to everything."

—Leonardo da Vinci

Take the time to nourish your body, calm your mind, and restore your gut because every part of you matters!

CHAPTER 7

From Mouth to Body: The Oral Health Connection

"There is no health without oral health."

—World Health Organization

One Saturday night when I was sixteen, my date was late and my younger cousins were at our house visiting. They were playing outside in the dark with my younger sister and begged me to join them. Fifty years later, I remember my mother's fateful words, "Go play with them. It won't hurt you." Oh, how wrong she was! A playful moment with my sister turned into a dental nightmare that would haunt me for the next five decades...

Coming around the corner of the house from opposite directions, my teeth collided with my sister's forehead. She ended up with part of one of my teeth in her forehead and a few stitches. I wasn't so lucky. The collision pushed my teeth way back in my mouth. The doctor at the emergency room wouldn't touch me and our family dentist was out of town for the weekend.

Our dentist saw me on that Sunday afternoon when he returned. He pulled my teeth back into place, which was much more painful after all the blood and bruising set in. He repaired the chip that went into my sister's head and explained to my mother and me that because the teeth didn't get pulled back into place right away, they probably wouldn't survive. The roots would likely die.

And die they did. The dentist advised us that a bridge wasn't an option because it involved both front teeth and that I would need root canals and crowns. One of the roots had broken off and required a post to secure the crown. We saw this as a way to save my teeth and my smile, and after a lot of work, my dentist made them look beautiful.

Little did we know then that those root canals were a ticking time bomb in my mouth, silently impacting my health in ways I wouldn't understand for decades. How could something in my teeth affect my gut, brain, and even my bones? The answer lies in the connections that science is only beginning to unravel.

The Mouth-Body Connection: More Than Just a Smile

Our mouths are intricately connected to our entire body. According to Traditional Chinese Medicine (TCM), each tooth links to specific organs and body systems through energy pathways called meridians. This ancient concept suggests a network that affects digestion, immune function, sleep, metabolism, and even heart health.

The oral cavity has its own microbiome—a unique community of microorganisms. Oral health isn't just about clean teeth; it's about maintaining a balanced microbiome, which helps to prevent chronic inflammation and support overall health.

While conventional dentistry has made progress in oral hygiene, it often overlooks these connections. The use of toxic metals and fluoride in dentistry raises concerns about systemic effects. Fluoride, promoted for cavity prevention, has been linked to reduced IQ in children. Procedures like root canals, which leave dead tissue in the body, may not fully consider broader health implications.

While preserving teeth is important, certain conventional practices like amalgam (mercury) fillings and leaving dead teeth in place may not be ideal. To truly care for our teeth, we need to understand the daily processes occurring in our mouths.

The Balance Between Remineralization and Demineralization

Teeth are dynamic structures composed of layers: translucent enamel, dentin with microscopic tubules, and innermost pulp containing blood vessels and nerves.

Tooth Anatomy

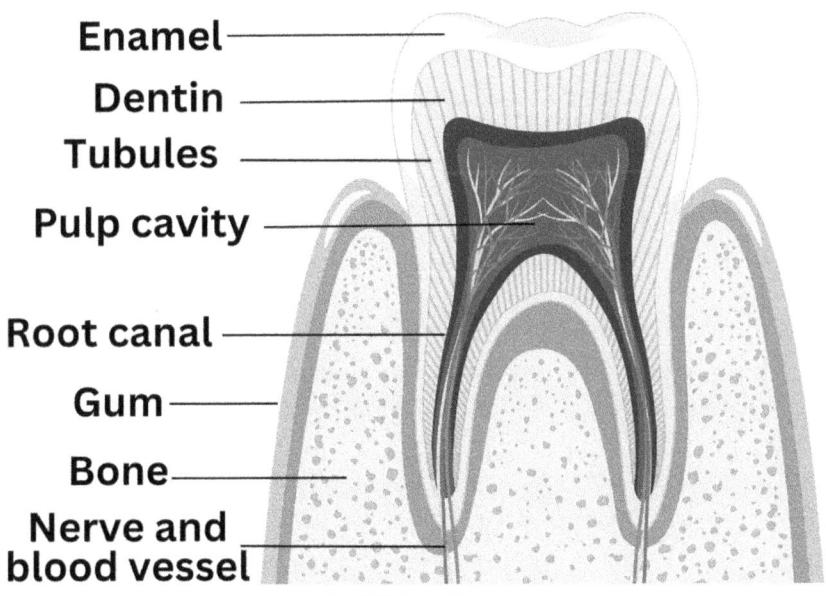

Enamel

Dentin

Tubules

Pulp cavity

Root canal

Gum

Bone

Nerve and blood vessel

© 2025 Terri Ward

These living structures constantly balance remineralization (repair) and demineralization (breakdown).

Remineralization is the natural repair process of restoring minerals to the enamel. It's supported by a healthy oral environment with adequate saliva, balanced pH, and sufficient minerals. A nutrient-dense diet, good oral hygiene, and practices that support beneficial oral bacteria, such as those discussed in this chapter, all contribute to this process.

Demineralization occurs when our teeth lose minerals like calcium and phosphate. An acidic oral environment accelerates this process, caused by diet, lifestyle, and health factors. Sugar and ultra-processed foods feed harmful bacteria that produce acid. Dry mouth, acid reflux, and mouth breathing contribute by reducing protective saliva flow.

As vinegar to the teeth and smoke to the eyes,
so are sluggards to those who send them.

(Proverbs 10:26 *NIV*)

Scripture uses the effects of acid on teeth as a metaphor for irritation and discomfort. The damage isn't just metaphorical—prolonged exposure to acid in our diets can cause real damage.

This Remin-Demin balance is influenced by diet, oral care, and even breathing habits. The accompanying infographic illustrates key factors affecting this balance.

Understanding this balance is crucial because teeth can self-repair under the right conditions, primarily with early-stage enamel damage. Repair occurs in an environment that favors remineralization, and nutrition plays a vital role in creating such an environment. Once decay reaches the dentin, professional treatment becomes necessary.

Remin-Demin

Calcium Phosphate   Calcium Phosphate

Ca   PO4   Ca   PO4

Saliva   Acid

Remineralization
- Saliva
- pH balance
- Xylitol
- Calcium & phosphate
- Vitamin D3
- Brushing & flossing

Demineralization
- Dry mouth
- Microbial imbalance
- Acid reflux
- Sugar & starches
- Mouth breathing
- Poor oral hygiene

© 2025 Terri Ward

The Role of Nutrition in Dental Health

Cavities result from an imbalance between sugar, bacteria, plaque, and nutritional deficiencies. Strong teeth and healthy gums rely on a steady supply of vitamins and essential minerals for enamel strength, saliva composition, and gum integrity.

Both sugar and high-glycemic starchy foods pose risks, increasing acid production in the mouth. These same foods are also linked to chronic conditions like type 2 diabetes and cardiovascular disease.

Key nutrients for oral and dental health and their sources include:

- **Calcium:** Full-fat dairy, sardines, wild-caught fish with edible bones, leafy greens.
- **Phosphorus:** Meat, fish, nuts, seeds.
- **Magnesium:** Nuts, seeds, legumes, leafy greens.
- **Vitamin A:** Liver, egg yolks, orange vegetables.
- **B vitamins:** Wild-caught salmon, organ meats, leafy greens, eggs.
- **Vitamin C:** Non-acidic sources like bell peppers, strawberries, broccoli, leafy greens.
- **Collagen:** Bone broth, slow-cooked meat dishes, fish with edible bones.
- **Vitamin D:** Sun exposure, liver, wild-caught salmon, sardines, or mackerel.
- **Vitamin K2:** Grass-fed butter and ghee, organ meats, fermented dairy.
- **Vitamin E:** Sunflower seeds, nuts, mango, avocado.

Phytic acid in grains, nuts, seeds, and legumes can block mineral absorption. Preparation methods like soaking, sprouting, and fermenting can reduce phytic acid levels and improve nutrient availability.

Prenatal nutrition is crucial for fetal dental development. Deficiencies in calcium, vitamin D, vitamin K2, and phosphorus during pregnancy can lead to weakened enamel and an increased risk of future dental issues. Breastfeeding supports proper jaw and palate alignment.

However, both breast milk and infant formula contain sugars that can cause tooth decay without proper hygiene or if milk pools in the mouth during sleep.

Understanding nutrition's role in dental health empowers us to make intentional choices supporting strong teeth and gums from the earliest stages of life. However, nutrition is just one part of the equation; the microorganisms in our mouths also play a role in cavity prevention and oral health.

The Oral Microbiome's Role in Oral Health

Your mouth is home to a bustling ecosystem of microbes that interact with your teeth, gums, tongue, and saliva to either protect or harm your oral health.

When balanced, beneficial bacteria neutralize acids to balance pH, prevent harmful bacterial overgrowth, and support enamel remineralization. Conversely, when the balance tips to favor harmful bacteria, acids erode tooth enamel, create plaque buildup, and inflame gum tissue. An acidic environment becomes a breeding ground for tooth decay, gum disease, and systemic inflammation.

This delicate balance can be disrupted by factors like antiseptic mouthwashes, especially those containing chlorhexidine. These can kill both harmful and beneficial bacteria, altering composition and reducing diversity. In contrast, microbiome-friendly rinses are alcohol-free and contain ingredients that support oral health without harming beneficial bacteria (see the Resources).

The Role of Saliva

Saliva does far more than just keep your mouth moist and aid in digestion. Saliva's key functions in maintaining oral health include:

- **Neutralizing acids:** Bicarbonate ions help buffer acids from food and bacterial activity, preventing enamel erosion.
- **Delivering minerals:** Calcium and phosphate ions in saliva support tooth remineralization, repairing early damage to enamel.
- **Controlling bacteria:** Saliva contains antimicrobial proteins, such as histatins, lactoferrin, and lysozyme, which help prevent harmful bacterial overgrowth.
- **Facilitating tissue repair:** Growth factors in saliva support rapid tissue healing, often without scarring.
- **Washing away debris:** Saliva helps clear food particles and sugars from the teeth and gums, reducing bacterial fuel sources.

Adequate hydration, nutrient-rich foods, and thorough chewing support healthy saliva flow. Limiting snacking and allowing time between meals allows saliva to restore pH balance and support remineralization.

The Importance of Gum Health

While saliva plays a key role in maintaining a healthy oral environment, your gums (*gingiva*) act as the foundation, keeping your teeth anchored and shielded from harmful bacteria. This soft tissue forms a protective seal around each tooth, acting as a barrier between your mouth and deeper tissues, including tooth roots and even your bloodstream.

This seal is critical because your oral cavity is exposed to bacteria all day long—through eating, drinking, speaking, and even breathing. At night, your body naturally produces less saliva. Breathing through your mouth further dries out the saliva and reduces its protective effects. This creates a dry mouth that weakens the protective seal, increasing the risk of tooth decay and gum problems.

Gum recession also weakens this seal, exposing tooth roots and creating pathways for harmful bacteria, toxins, and debris to infiltrate deeper tissues and even the bloodstream.

Left unchecked, this infiltration can lead to decay, infection, and periodontal disease. But the consequences don't stop there. The bacteria can travel through the bloodstream to other areas of the body. Research shows certain bacterial strains can cross the blood-brain barrier, contributing to the formation of plaques and tangles associated with Alzheimer's disease. Periodontal disease has also been linked to cardiovascular disease and metabolic disorders.

Maintaining optimal gum health goes beyond gentle brushing and flossing. It's about creating an environment where beneficial bacteria thrive, saliva production remains steady, and inflammation is kept in check.

Root Canals: The Silent Thief

When infections progress deep into the root and bone, they can lead to significant damage, often requiring invasive treatments like root canals—procedures that come with their own set of risks.

Root canals have been compared to taxidermy because they leave dead tissue in the body—a practice unacceptable in any other medical field. The procedure removes the nerve, eliminating pain, but leaves tubules where bacteria and toxins can thrive.

With blood and nerve supply cut off, the immune system can't effectively fight infection. These bacteria and their toxins can enter the bloodstream, potentially affecting the heart, brain, and immune system.

Regardless of how expertly a root canal is performed, fully sterilizing the root canal system is impossible. Research indicates that root canal-treated teeth harbor anaerobic bacteria capable of releasing potent biotoxins that drive chronic inflammation and systemic illness. Studies identify these bacterial toxins as some of the most severe biotoxins in nature.

The consequences extend beyond oral health. Studies show that 97 to 98% of women diagnosed with breast cancer between ages 30 and 70 had a history of root canals or other dental infections on the same side as their cancer. Thermographic imaging supports this link, revealing heat spots in the jaw of 95% of breast cancer patients, mirroring the side of their malignancy.

In the early 20th century, Dr. Weston A. Price, a pioneer in dental health research, noticed his patients often became ill after root canals. In his research, he removed root canal-treated teeth from sick patients, sterilized them, and implanted them under rabbits' skin. He found that the rabbits developed the same illness as the patient—whether heart disease, kidney disease, or neurological disorders. The same tooth implanted into fifty rabbits caused the same condition as the original patient.

Despite Price's findings, modern dentistry has largely dismissed concerns about lingering infections in root canal-treated teeth. Most dentists rely on two-dimensional X-rays, which lack the depth perception needed to detect silent abscesses or bone infections, leaving many infections undiagnosed. Cone Beam Computed Tomography (CBCT), an advanced 3D imaging technology, can reveal these hidden infections that standard X-rays often miss.

Root canals remain a significant blind spot in both dentistry and medicine, yet their effects can ripple through every system in the body. Recognizing their systemic risks and using tools like CBCT scans for detection are critical steps in addressing chronic health challenges.

While some dental issues require professional intervention, there's much you can do daily to protect and support your oral health.

Practical Steps for Supporting Oral Health

Our teeth were designed to last a lifetime, but our modern lifestyles demand intentional care to ensure they do. Every choice we make—what we eat, how we clean our teeth, the products we use, and the habits we form—affects their strength and longevity.

The simple, low or no-cost steps below can support your teeth, gums, and overall oral microbiome. These steps aren't about perfection but about building consistent habits that align with how our bodies are designed to function.

1. **Stay Hydrated.** Drink water throughout the day to maintain healthy saliva production. Saliva is your mouth's natural defense: it neutralizes acids, washes away food particles, and delivers essential minerals like calcium and phosphate to your teeth.

2. **Use Mineral-Rich Toothpaste or Tooth Powder.** Opt for toothpaste or tooth powder with hydroxyapatite or other remineralizing agents. Avoid products with harsh chemicals like sodium lauryl sulfate (SLS) or glycerin, which can disrupt remineralization.

3. **Incorporate Oil Pulling into Your Routine.** Swish a tablespoon of coconut oil in your mouth for 10 to 15 minutes; then spit it out (not into the sink, as the oil can solidify and clog pipes). This practice may reduce harmful bacteria, support gum health, and freshen breath.

4. **Switch to Microbiome-Friendly Rinses.** Swap antiseptic mouthwash for an alcohol-free rinse with natural ingredients that support a healthy oral microbiome.

5. **Support Oral Health Through Nutrition.** Eat a nutrient-dense diet rich in vitamins A, D, and K2, along with calcium, phosphorus, and magnesium. Include fermented foods and prebiotics to nourish beneficial bacteria in your mouth and gut.

6. **Address Mouth Breathing.** Breathing through your mouth (especially at night), dries out saliva and creates an environment where harmful bacteria thrive. If your nose breathing isn't constricted, consider mouth taping while sleeping.

For links to products, including remineralizing toothpaste and microbiome-friendly mouth rinses, check the Resources.

Choosing Healing, Finding Gratitude

Over the years following my collision with my sister, I had a post inserted in the other tooth to secure the second crown. Both crowns were replaced multiple times, with restorations and even abscess surgery. I was determined to save my teeth.

After hearing Dr. Griffin Cole, former president of the International Academy of Oral Medicine and Toxicology, speak at a Nutritional Therapy Association conference, he advised me to remove my amalgams and root canals. I had the amalgams safely removed by a holistic dentist but had several excuses for avoiding the extractions. In reality, it was vanity. My teeth looked good, and I feared having a missing tooth or unsightly replacements.

Fifty years post-root canals, new health issues emerged. My already highly reactive immune system became even more overprotective, and labs suggested systemic candida overgrowth. A functional medicine doctor explained that root canals, especially in the upper jaw, can create ideal conditions for candida in the sinuses. He urged a CBCT scan at a biological or holistic dentist's office.

Fortunately, my biological dentist, Dr. Luke Jacobsen, has CBCT technology that many conventional dentists still do not offer. While X-rays taken in May showed no issues, by August the CBCT revealed an abscess eating into my jawbone. My root canals had to go.

I scheduled extractions and implants but overheard the staff discussing someone rejecting an implant. I remembered someone else I knew had experienced the same thing. Given how reactive my immune system was, I told Dr. Jacobsen I didn't trust my body not to reject them. He said, "Neither do I." Plan B: a bridge.

After a series of appointments, I now have a bridge that looks better than my crowns. Initially, the bridge felt foreign and uncomfortable. One day, I encountered a store clerk who was missing his two front teeth. I immediately said a prayer for him and asked God for forgiveness for being ungrateful. I am truly grateful to no longer have dead teeth in my mouth poisoning me and for the ability to choose a path of healing.

I'm also grateful for the knowledge that led me to a skilled and compassionate biological dentist. Biological dentists use biologically friendly materials, typically avoid mercury, fluoride, and root canals, and follow special safety protocols with advanced equipment for amalgam removal. Finding a biological dentist is well worth the effort, even if it means traveling. A directory for finding these dentists is linked in the Resources.

Giving thanks always for everything to God the Father
in the name of our Lord Jesus Christ.

(Ephesians 5:20 *CSB*)

CHAPTER 8

Strong Foundations: The Bone-Body Connection

The Lord will always lead you, satisfy you in a parched land, and strengthen your bones. You will be like a watered garden and like a spring whose water never runs dry.

(Isaiah 58:11 CSB)

When I was 14, I broke my arm playing basketball. It wasn't a minor injury—it was clearly broken, so displaced that I needed anesthesia just to have it set. I woke up with my arm in traction, where it stayed for two days.

The doctor said it would heal in six weeks, but when six weeks passed, my bone still wasn't healed. Every couple of weeks, I returned for another X-ray only to hear, "Not yet. Come back in two weeks." Frustrated, I began to question my doctor's competence. Looking back now, I realize the issue wasn't the doctor—it was my gut health.

I likely had undiagnosed celiac disease or a severe gluten sensitivity for most of my life. My gastroenterologist later agreed this was probably the cause of my long-term health issues. As a kid, I often got nosebleeds, canker sores, migraines, and stomach pain—all signs of celiac disease. I thought stomach pain was just a normal part of life. I never spoke up about it after seeing people make fun of my cousin for going to the emergency room for "gas pains."

My short stature should have been another clue. Short stature is strongly linked to celiac disease in children. When the intestine is damaged, the body can't absorb nutrients needed for growth and bone healing. Like my other symptoms, it was another piece of the puzzle that no one connected.

Celiac disease can silently weaken bones. Research shows that people with untreated celiac disease have lower bone density and a higher risk of osteoporosis, even without obvious digestive symptoms. Despite a celiac prevalence of 3.4% in those with osteoporosis, celiac testing is rare. Instead, osteoporosis is often considered part of normal aging and treated without investigating underlying causes.

If bones become weak, there's an underlying reason that should be identified and addressed. Like your teeth, your bones were designed to last a lifetime with proper care. Understanding the root causes of bone weakness is the first step to reclaiming their strength.

Understanding Bone Health

Strong bones are more than a safeguard against fractures—they enable us to live vibrant, active lives. Our physical health affects how we steward the time, energy, and resources God has given us. By understanding and caring for our bones, we equip ourselves to better fulfill our earthly missions and serve those around us.

Bones are not static structures. They are living, dynamic tissues with multiple roles, and are in a continuous state of remodeling.

Bone remodeling involves cells called osteoblasts that form new bone and osteoclasts that break down old bone. This process allows bones to adapt, repair damage, and maintain strength. It also helps control the body's biochemical balance. When blood calcium levels drop, osteoclasts are triggered to release calcium from bone. However, if more minerals are removed than are replaced, osteoporosis can develop.

Bone Remodeling

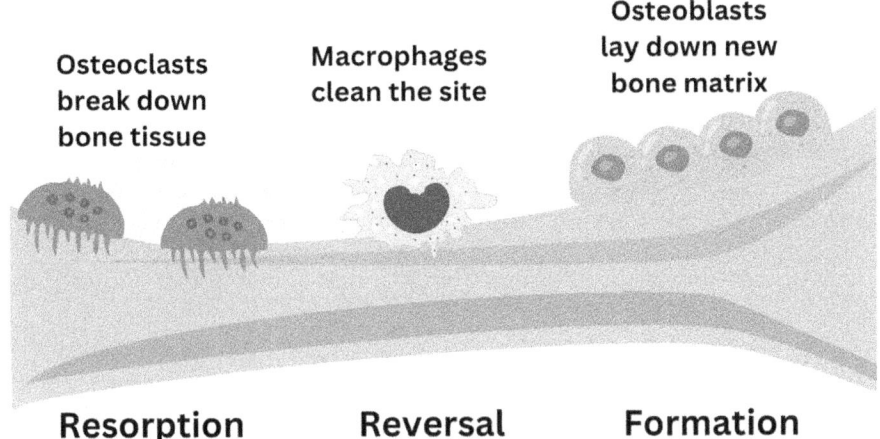

Osteoclasts break down bone tissue

Macrophages clean the site

Osteoblasts lay down new bone matrix

Resorption   **Reversal**   **Formation**

© 2025 Terri Ward

At the core of bone health is the collagen matrix, which provides flexibility and strength to the bone. The bone marrow, in the bone cavity, supports immune cell production and essential metabolic processes.

Healthy bones are crucial for overall well-being, contributing to:

- **Immune Function:** Bone marrow produces white blood cells vital for fighting infections.
- **Metabolic Regulation:** Bones store and release calcium and phosphate to maintain balance in the blood and to support muscle contractions, nerve signaling, and other vital functions.
- **Overall Stability:** Bones form the foundation for movement and posture. Weak bones can impair mobility, balance, and quality of life.

Bone health changes throughout life. Bones grow rapidly during childhood and adolescence, with density peaking by age 30. In adulthood, hormones shift. Women lose bone rapidly after menopause due to low estrogen, while men experience gradual loss as testosterone declines. Early action is key to maintaining strong bones.

Key Risk Factors for Osteoporosis

One in two women and up to one in four men over the age of 50 in the U.S. will break a bone due to osteoporosis. With hip fractures, 25% die within a year of injury and another 25% move to a nursing home. Of the remaining 50%, only 15% regain the ability to walk across a room unassisted six months later.

Our ancestors had strong bones throughout their lives, and many people in non-industrialized regions still do today. So, why is osteoporosis so prevalent and occurring earlier in life now? What has changed?

If women begin losing bone before menopause, and estrogen therapy doesn't always stop the loss, then estrogen isn't the only factor involved. Factors that increase the likelihood of osteoporosis include:

- **Advancing age:** Risk rises with age; men typically experience bone loss later than women.
- **Gender:** Women lose more bone mass and have a higher risk with a history of depression or prolonged menstrual irregularities.
- **Genetics and family history:** Osteoporosis in mother or grandmother, or a genetic predisposition.
- **Ethnicity:** European or Asian descent.
- **Body composition:** Body mass index (BMI) 19 or less; height loss.

- **Hormonal factors:** Low estrogen or testosterone, premature menopause or hysterectomy, overactive thyroid or parathyroid gland, pituitary disorders (e.g., Cushing's syndrome).

- **Medical conditions:** Rheumatoid arthritis, eating disorders, metabolic acidosis, kidney disease, diabetes, dementia, gastrointestinal malabsorption (e.g., celiac or Crohn's disease, small intestinal bacterial overgrowth).

- **Lifestyle factors:** Insufficient exercise, limited sun exposure, emotional stress, smoking, alcohol or caffeine (more than two drinks per day).

- **Medications:** Long-term steroid use, excess thyroid hormone, benzodiazepines.

- **History of fractures or falls:** Personal or parental history of fractures in later life, or a history of falls.

- **Dietary factors:** Low calcium intake, very high or low protein or phosphorus consumption.

While these factors increase the risk of osteoporosis, they don't guarantee it will happen. Multiple factors are likely involved—many of which are within our control to change.

Key Nutrients for Bone Health

Calcium is widely recognized as essential for strong bones, as it is a major structural component of bone tissue. For optimal bone health, a daily intake of 1,000 to 1,200 mg is typically recommended for adults. Ideally, this amount should come from food, because supplemental calcium may end up in the arteries instead of the bones.

Studies show that calcium supplementation not only fails to prevent or treat osteoporosis or reduce fracture risk, but may also increase cardiovascular risk, especially in older adults. Getting enough calcium from food is a safer and more effective approach. Supplements should be reserved for confirmed calcium deficiencies and always combined with vitamin D3 and K2 to help the body use calcium properly and reduce the risk of arterial calcification.

While dairy is a common calcium source, it's neither the only nor necessarily the best option—despite what we've long been taught. Many people have been led to believe that without regular milk consumption, bones won't grow strong or stay healthy. Yet countless cultures have built and maintained strong bones without relying on dairy as a staple. For a practical example, check the Resources for a sample meal plan that meets daily calcium needs without dairy.

Whole, nutrient-rich foods can provide plenty of calcium, along with the co-factors needed for absorption and bone strength, potentially lowering calcium needs. For strong bones, your body needs a variety of nutrients working together.

Below are the key nutrients involved in bone metabolism and some of their whole food sources:

- **Protein:** Meat, fish, seafood, dairy, eggs, legumes, bone broth, collagen powder.
- **Boron:** Prunes, raisins, dried apricots, avocados, nuts.
- **Calcium:** Dairy, sardines, leafy greens, sesame seeds.
- **Copper:** Liver, oysters, nuts, seeds, dark chocolate.
- **Iron:** Red meat, spinach, lentils, fortified cereals.
- **Magnesium:** Nuts, seeds, legumes, leafy greens, whole grains.
- **Manganese:** Whole grains, nuts, leafy green vegetables, tea.
- **Phosphorus:** Dairy products, meat, fish, eggs, nuts, legumes.
- **Potassium:** Bananas, potatoes, leafy greens, beans, yogurt.
- **Silicon:** Whole grains, carrots, green beans, beer.
- **Zinc:** Beef, shrimp, spinach, flaxseeds, oysters, pumpkin seeds.

- **Vitamins B6, B12, folate:** Whole grains, meat, eggs, legumes, nuts, seeds, leafy greens.
- **Vitamin C:** Citrus fruits, berries, bell peppers, broccoli, potatoes.
- **Vitamin D:** Sun exposure, liver, wild-caught fish (salmon, sardines, herring, mackerel), egg yolks, fortified foods (milk, orange juice).
- **Vitamin K:** Dark green vegetables (spinach, kale, cabbage), eggs, kiwi fruit, fermented foods (cheese, natto).

Many Americans fall short of the Estimated Average Requirement (EAR) for these nutrients. For example, among those aged four years and older:

- 44.1% don't get enough calcium.
- 52.2% fall short on magnesium.
- 51% consume too little vitamin K.
- 94.3% get insufficient vitamin D, which depends heavily on sunlight exposure—a factor many people overlook in bone health.

The Role of Sunlight in Bone Health

But for you who revere my name, the sun of righteousness will rise with healing in its rays.

(Malachi 4:2 *NIV*)

God gave us the sun for more than light. Scripture highlights its healing power in Malachi 4:2. Yet many of us spend too much time indoors or use toxic sunscreens when outdoors.

Vitamin D, technically a hormone, is best absorbed through sun exposure. I struggled for years to raise my vitamin D levels with supplements alone. It wasn't until I spent hours outdoors landscaping our yard that my levels improved.

Historically, hospitals prioritized outdoor time for patients. They recognized the restorative power of sunlight—a practice supported by modern science. Sunlight promotes healing, enhances mood and thinking, and improves overall health.

In winter or at higher latitudes, UVB rays for vitamin D synthesis are scarce. For chronically low vitamin D levels or poor supplement response, consider brief UVB tanning bed sessions (up to 10 minutes, five days a week). While this may seem unconventional, the risks of low vitamin D—like weakened immunity and higher cancer risk—are serious. Consult your healthcare provider about safe and moderate sun exposure options.

Sun exposure also helps regulate sleep by influencing melatonin production and boosts calcium absorption. However, effective calcium absorption and bone health depend on gut health. Without a well-functioning digestive system, even the best diet and supplements can fall short. This brings us to another critical connection: the gut-bone connection.

The Gut-Bone Connection

Gut and bone health are deeply interconnected. A healthy gut supports nutrient absorption, controls inflammation, and influences bone metabolism. In turn, bones release hormones like osteocalcin, which may impact gut function and microbial balance.

When the gut lining becomes leaky, toxins and undigested food particles can enter the bloodstream. This can trigger inflammation that disrupts the balance between bone breakdown and formation.

Beneficial gut bacteria like Lactobacillus and Bifidobacterium enhance calcium, magnesium, and phosphorus absorption. Prebiotics, such as inulin and fructooligosaccharides (FOS), feed these bacteria and promote the production of short-chain fatty acids (SCFAs).

SCFAs nourish colon cells and strengthen the gut barrier to reduce permeability. They lower intestinal pH to improve calcium solubility. SCFAs also reduce immune responses and inflammation to support bone remodeling.

A balanced gut microbiome supports bone health by reducing inflammation, improving mineral absorption, and strengthening the gut lining. At the same time, osteocalcin from bones may support the microbiome, highlighting the gut-bone connection and how each relies on the other.

Hormone Replacement Therapy (HRT)

HRT is often considered for preventing osteoporosis, especially in women during and after menopause, when estrogen levels decline. Estrogen helps maintain bone mineral density (BMD) by slowing bone resorption, but not all forms of HRT are the same.

Conventional HRT

Conventional HRT typically uses synthetic hormones like conjugated equine estrogens or ethinyl estradiol. Synthetic progesterone is often added to reduce the risk of endometrial cancer. These hormones are linked to higher risks of certain cancers and cardiovascular issues and may be poorly tolerated.

Bioidentical Hormone Replacement Therapy (BHRT)

BHRT uses hormones identical to those produced by the body, including estriol—a gentler, safer estrogen—along with bioidentical progesterone, DHEA, and testosterone. This personalized approach balances multiple hormones, recognizing that estrogen works in concert with the others to support bone health.

HRT and BHRT are available in various forms, including oral tablets, patches, gels, creams, vaginal rings, and suppositories. Choosing the right method depends on individual needs and should be guided by an experienced practitioner.

Test, Don't Guess

Accurate hormone testing is essential for safe and effective treatment. While blood tests are common, saliva testing often better reflects active hormone levels, especially for steroid hormones like progesterone and testosterone. Testing ensures personalized treatment, avoiding under- or over-dosing.

Hormones are interconnected, and a personalized approach that balances estrogen, progesterone, DHEA, and testosterone is key to optimizing bone and overall health. When one hormone is out of balance, it can disrupt the entire system. Hormonal balance can support stronger bones and improve overall quality of life.

A Note on Medications

Medications are often prescribed for osteoporosis, aiming either to slow bone loss (antiresorptive drugs) or to stimulate new bone growth (anabolic drugs). Common examples include bisphosphonates (like Fosamax), denosumab, selective estrogen receptor modulators (SERMs), teriparatide, abaloparatide, and romosozumab.

Bisphosphonates work by inhibiting osteoclasts, the cells that break down bone. This also prevents the removal of old, micro-damaged bone, which makes bones appear denser on scans and results in a higher BMD measure. However, this old bone is more brittle and prone to fractures.

Other medications have similar trade-offs. Denosumab slows bone loss but can cause rapid declines in density if stopped abruptly. Anabolic drugs like teriparatide stimulate new bone growth but are usually reserved for severe cases and limited to short-term use due to potential risks, including a higher incidence of bone cancer (osteosarcoma) seen in animal studies.

While these medications may slightly lower the risk of fractures, the overall benefit is modest. In medicine, the effectiveness of a treatment is often described using the "number needed to treat," which means how many people must be treated for one person to benefit. For bisphosphonates, at least 91 people need to be treated for three years to prevent just one hip fracture—an outcome considered a very poor result.

Meanwhile, the risks—including fractures of the thighbone that can happen with little or no trauma (known as atypical femoral fractures) and jawbone damage—become more likely after three to five years of continuous treatment.

Given the modest benefits and real risks of medications, it's important to be informed and discuss all options thoroughly with your healthcare practitioner. Building stronger bones requires a holistic approach—restoring hormonal balance, consuming the right nutrients, and incorporating intentional, weight-bearing movement.

Weight-Bearing Exercise: A Non-Negotiable for Bone Health

Tendons connect bones and muscles, and when muscles contract, they exert force on the bones they're anchored to. This force makes both the muscle and bones stronger. Weight-bearing and resistance exercises stimulate osteoblasts to build bone, increasing density and resilience. Interestingly, stress on a leg bone can help strengthen the spine and shoulders, and even light weightlifting while seated can be beneficial.

Without regular movement and stress, bones weaken over time. Since BMD peaks around age 30, maintaining it through consistent activity is vital. Walking, hiking, resistance training, yoga, and Pilates promote stronger bones. These activities also improve muscle strength, posture, and balance, reducing the risk of falls and fractures as we age.

Other benefits of exercise include improved cognitive function, mood, energy, and confidence. Physical activity increases Brain-Derived Neurotrophic Factor (BDNF), a protein that supports memory, learning, and neuroplasticity—the brain's ability to adapt and form new connections—while reducing the risk of neurodegenerative diseases.

Remember, "Use it or lose it."

Action Steps for Stronger Bones

Improving bone health doesn't have to be overwhelming. Start with one simple step and gradually incorporate others into your routine. Remember, small, consistent changes can lead to huge improvements over time.

1. **Know Your Bone Status.** Request a DEXA scan and Trabecular Bone Score (TBS) from your healthcare provider. Ask for the full printout. Consider additional tests including urine or serum bone turnover markers and a serum or hair mineral analysis.

2. **Prioritize a Nutrient-Dense, Anti-Inflammatory Diet.** Focus on dark leafy greens, bone broth, nuts, seeds, high-quality proteins, and healthy fats.

3. **Know Your Vitamin D Status.** Get a 25-hydroxyvitamin D test through your healthcare provider or a direct-to-consumer lab.

4. **Incorporate Weight-Bearing and Resistance Exercises.** Choose enjoyable activities like walking, dancing, or weightlifting that you'll do consistently.

5. **Customize Your Supplementation Strategy.** Work with a knowledgeable practitioner to assess nutrient levels and design a personalized plan.

The steps we take to protect and strengthen our bones today are an investment in a longer health span.

Reflections and Lessons Learned

When I broke my wrist in 2020, the healing difference was striking. Decades earlier, my broken arm had been slow to heal, but this time, my recovery was right on track and healed fully in six weeks. However, the X-rays revealed that just six weeks of not moving my wrist caused a visible decrease in bone density. Changes like this are usually only detectable with a DEXA scan. It was a powerful reminder of how much our bones depend on consistent movement for strength.

A follow-up DEXA scan confirmed I had osteoporosis. Reflecting on this, I couldn't help but ponder the hidden factors that influence bone health. My likely undiagnosed celiac disease may have weakened my bones in the past, but I also discovered another invisible burden: uranium toxicity. This toxic heavy metal disrupts bone health by slowing new bone formation, speeding up bone breakdown, and causing the loss of calcium and phosphate through urine.

These experiences reminded me that bone health isn't just about age, calcium, or estrogen. It's about uncovering deeper influences—like malabsorption and environmental exposures—that silently rob us of our strength.

What hidden factors might be silently affecting your bone health, and how can you begin uncovering them today?

Lifetime bone health is possible, and it's never too late or too early to start building strong bones. The question is, are you willing to look beyond the surface and address the root causes of bone loss?

CHAPTER 9

The Inflammation Connection: A Modern Epidemic

"Every choice we make, from our diet to our environment, either fuels or fights inflammation."

—Author Unknown

Several years ago, my husband was scheduled a few months out for surgery to treat achalasia, an autoimmune esophageal disorder that progressively impairs swallowing. In the interim, he took a celebratory trip back east with his daughter, eating indulgent fare like lobster and Ben & Jerry's ice cream. Upon his return, his symptoms took a terrifying turn. He suddenly couldn't even swallow his own saliva!

We went to a nearby emergency room (ER) for what should have been a straightforward procedure: placing a nasogastric (N-G) tube. An N-G tube is a thin tube inserted through the nose into the stomach to relieve pressure or deliver nutrition. Unfortunately, what followed was anything but straightforward.

The medical system failed us at every turn. Despite my protests, he was given unnecessary medications and not an N-G tube. He was admitted to the hospital and underwent a different procedure, which was botched, leaving him in excruciating pain. The resulting pain medications caused nausea, compounding his already serious condition.

After days deteriorating in the hospital, my husband finally got an N-G tube and was discharged. However, at home, he couldn't keep the tube down due to the nausea. While waiting for his surgeon's staff to discuss his situation and call me back, he started shaking with rigors. I took him to the hospital ER where his surgery was scheduled—still a week out. While I was checking him in, his eyes rolled back in his head, and he collapsed. The ER attendant grabbed his wheelchair and raced him back, yelling "Code Assist," which means 'All hands on deck.'

As her shouts faded, I was left wondering: Did he just die?

In that moment, everything else faded. I wasn't worried about his nutrition. All I could do was pray that he would survive.

During the months leading up to surgery, he lost weight due to swallowing difficulty. In the previous week or two before this ordeal, his swallowing worsened dramatically, and he had lost a third of his body weight. After days of medical mismanagement and no nutrition, his body reached its breaking point.

Looking back, I now see there was more at play than we realized.

His health crisis didn't happen overnight, and it wasn't due to bad luck. His body had been under siege long before that terrifying moment in the ER when he collapsed. Like so many others struggling with chronic illness, the real danger had been lurking beneath the surface—slowly wearing him down until one final trigger sent everything crashing down.

For millions, this same silent process is already at work in their bodies, depleting energy, weakening defenses, and setting the stage for disease. Yet, most people don't even realize it's happening. This harrowing experience opened my eyes to a broader health issue affecting countless lives.

Inflammation: A Vital Defense Mechanism

Imagine a silent threat lurking within us, impacting our longevity and vitality. This isn't about the cancer cells we all carry. It's something even more pervasive: inflammation. For years, inflammation flew under the radar, but the COVID-19 pandemic's deadly cytokine storms thrust it into the spotlight, revealing how it can wreak havoc on our bodies.

Inflammation is both friend and foe. It's vital for healing injury or fighting infection when temporary, but a silent killer when chronic. It becomes chronic when the immune system perceives an ongoing threat. Today, this threat is everywhere—triggered by stress, poor sleep, hormonal imbalances, and even air pollution—making inflammation a modern epidemic. To understand how inflammation becomes chronic, let's first look at how inflammation should work.

When we encounter injury, infection, or foreign substances, acute inflammation is the body's initial response. It triggers redness, swelling, heat, and pain as the immune system rushes to the affected area to fight off threats and initiate healing. This type of inflammation is natural, beneficial, and necessary. Once the threat is neutralized, the immune system should calm down.

However, sometimes the immune system doesn't calm down and stays on high alert even when there's no obvious injury or infection. This leads to chronic inflammation, resulting in persistent, smoldering inflammation. This keeps immune cells actively releasing proteins that cause collateral damage to nearby tissues and organs over time. It's like having an army of repair crews that keep demolishing instead of fixing.

As the body tries to heal the inflammation-induced damage, it lays down scar tissue. Scar tissue is inferior to healthy tissue, so function becomes impaired. Imagine trying to repair a road by just paving over the potholes instead of filling them first.

This cycle of damage, failed healing, and scarring can last for years, slowly degrading the affected organs and systems. Chronic diseases like heart disease, cancer, rheumatoid arthritis, and Alzheimer's may result as inflammation continuously attacks tissues.

Modern Lifestyle and Inflammatory Triggers

Our modern world looks nothing like the world our ancestors lived in. Today, artificial light disrupts sleep, environmental toxins disrupt our hormones, and our diets and inactive lifestyles strain our bodies. All of this constantly triggers inflammation throughout our bodies. To stay healthy, it's important to understand what causes this inflammation.

The main sources of inflammation in our daily lives fall into these categories:

- **Lifestyle:** Poor sleep, sedentary behavior, smoking, alcohol consumption, chronic stress.
- **Diet and Nutrition:** Sugar, gluten, processed foods, low-fiber intake, vitamin and mineral deficiencies (e.g., magnesium, vitamin D, vitamin E, zinc, and selenium), food allergies and sensitivities.
- **Mental and Emotional Health:** Stress, anxiety, trauma, adverse childhood events, social isolation, lack of social support.
- **Metabolic Health:** Obesity, insulin resistance, diabetes, metabolic syndrome.
- **Chronic Conditions:** Cardiovascular disease, chronic pain, hormonal imbalances, microbial infections.
- **Environmental Exposures:** Air pollution, heavy metals, chemical and mold exposure, socioeconomic determinants of health.
- **Biological Factors:** Aging factors, genetics.
- **Oral and Gut Health:** Gut microbiome imbalances, dental health issues.

Constant inflammatory triggers make it hard for the immune system to stay balanced. Ongoing, low-level inflammation can result, gradually weakening our defenses until we notice disease symptoms.

Recognizing Inflammation

Blood tests such as C-reactive protein (CRP), erythrocyte sedimentation rate (ESR), and interleukin-6 (IL-6) are useful for assessing and tracking inflammation levels. However, they may not always be utilized if symptoms aren't apparent. By being attentive and listening to our bodies, we can identify the clues they provide for early identification of issues.

On a daily basis, it's crucial to pay attention to these potential signs of underlying inflammation:

- Persistent fatigue and low energy levels
- Insomnia
- Brain fog and forgetfulness (signs of neuroinflammation)
- Muscle or overall body pain
- Weight gain or loss
- Digestive issues like acid reflux, diarrhea, or constipation
- Frequent infections
- Depression, anxiety, or other mood disorders

These seemingly minor annoyances might be your body alerting you to chronic inflammation. For example, feeling mentally foggy after certain meals could indicate inflammation from those foods. Even more concerning is that increased inflammation has been associated with impulsive thinking and suicidal thoughts.

To truly address the root cause of chronic inflammation, we need to delve deeper into one of its significant contributors: leaky gut.

Leaky Gut: The Gateway to Inflammation and Autoimmunity

"All disease begins in the gut."
—Hippocrates

"All disease begins in the (leaky) gut."
—Alessio Fasano, MD

Leaky gut isn't just a digestive issue; it's also a major trigger for chronic inflammation and autoimmunity. If you haven't already, refer back to chapter 6 for a breakdown of what weakens the gut barrier and how to repair it.

For individuals with a genetic predisposition to autoimmune disease, a leaky gut sets the stage for an immune system malfunction and chronic inflammation. This can be due to something called molecular mimicry. If leaked particles have molecular structures similar to body tissues, the immune system can become confused and attack its own cells.

This process of leaky gut and molecular mimicry can play a role in autoimmune conditions. For example, in Hashimoto's thyroiditis, the immune system may mistake the thyroid gland for gluten, triggering an attack. Similar mechanisms contribute to celiac disease, rheumatoid arthritis, lupus, and multiple sclerosis.

Addressing intestinal permeability is crucial for restoring gut health, calming the immune response, and breaking the cycle of inflammation.

The Inflammatory Epidemics Fueled by Modern Living

Our modern lifestyle choices fuel ongoing inflammation in our bodies. This leads to more health issues that not only shorten our lifespan but also reduce our health span—the years we stay in good health. Allergies are a good example of this trend. Once rare, they are now common due to an overactive immune system. The immune system mistakes harmless things like pollen or certain foods as threats, causing unnecessary inflammation.

Let's explore some common inflammatory conditions that are influenced by today's lifestyle and constant immune activation.

Insulin Resistance and Metabolic Syndrome

Insulin resistance, one of the conditions included in metabolic syndrome, is linked to chronic inflammation. It occurs when cells no longer respond properly to insulin, leaving sugar in the bloodstream and raising the risk of diabetes and organ damage.

Metabolic syndrome is a group of risk factors for type 2 diabetes, heart disease, and stroke. It's diagnosed when three or more of the following factors are present:

- Excess belly fat
- High blood sugar (insulin resistance)
- High triglycerides
- Low high-density lipoprotein (HDL) cholesterol
- High blood pressure

The most recent CDC data indicates that over 38 million Americans have diabetes, and 97 million have prediabetes. Among obese teens, more than half show signs of insulin resistance.

In addition, about 23% of U.S. adults have metabolic syndrome.

Obesity

Obesity, typically defined as a body mass index (BMI) of 30 or higher, involves both visceral fat around organs and subcutaneous fat under the skin. When there is too much of this fat, it promotes inflammation. Leptin, a hormone produced by fat cells, plays a key role in this process by regulating the immune system and promoting pro-inflammatory cytokines. Conditions linked to obesity, such as insulin resistance, metabolic syndrome, and nonalcoholic fatty liver disease (NAFLD), further increase inflammation.

CDC data indicates that as of 2020, 41.9% of U.S. adults and 19.7% of youth had obesity, with rates rising 3% during the pandemic. The trend is evident when comparing movies from 60 years ago or looking at old photos of people at the beach—each decade, the population has grown noticeably heavier.

Visceral Fat and the "Skinny Fat" Phenomenon

Visceral adipose tissue (VAT) accumulates around vital organs in the abdomen, including the stomach, intestines, liver, and pancreas. This type of fat is different from subcutaneous fat, which is located just underneath the skin. VAT is metabolically active. It produces hormones that regulate appetite and insulin sensitivity and releases inflammatory molecules. It is linked to an increased risk of chronic inflammatory conditions like insulin resistance, type 2 diabetes, heart disease, and NAFLD.

The term 'skinny fat' describes people with a normal weight but excess visceral fat. Despite looking thin, their disease risks from chronic inflammation match those with obesity.

Non-Alcoholic Fatty Liver Disease (NAFLD)

Once considered a rare condition, NAFLD now affects about 25% of the global population and 80 to 100 million people in the U.S. It is characterized by excessive fat in the liver that triggers inflammation. It can progress to more severe forms like non-alcoholic steatohepatitis (NASH), cirrhosis, and liver failure.

Cancer

Recent research shows that around 25% of all cancers are linked to chronic inflammation. Things like chronic infections and persistent inflammatory conditions create an environment that allows cancer to develop. These conditions damage DNA and help abnormal cells grow and survive. Cancers often tied to inflammation include colon, breast, prostate, lung, and liver.

Neurodegeneration Diseases

Chronic inflammation also affects our brain health and our ability to think clearly, reason, and form memories. It raises the risk of neuro-degenerative diseases like Alzheimer's and dementia, as well as milder cognitive issues. It can directly damage brain cells and tissues and neg-atively impact the brain in several ways:

- It can lead to the production of autoantibodies that bind to receptors and disrupt normal nerve signaling.
- It can contribute to the loss of myelin and changes in white matter, which are crucial for nerve function.
- It can contribute to the misfolding and buildup of proteins, such as amyloid and tau, linked to Alzheimer's.

Alzheimer's disease, the most common form of dementia, affects ap-proximately 6.9 million Americans over 65, with projections reaching 13 million by 2050. Death rates from Alzheimer's have nearly doubled in the past 20 years. Additionally, 11.1% of adults—about 1 in 9—experience subjective cognitive impairment, an early warning sign of Alzheimer's and related dementias.

Recent data suggests dementia is appearing at younger ages, with early-onset Alzheimer's cases rising worldwide. Each year, about 350,000 new cases of early-onset dementia are diagnosed globally.

Inflammaging and Accelerated Aging

Inflammaging refers to the chronic, low-level inflammation that accelerates the aging of cells, tissues, and organs. Persistent exposure to inflammatory triggers speeds up this process, increasing the risk of age-related diseases and conditions.

Inflammaging contributes to age-related conditions like cardiovascular disease, type 2 diabetes, arthritis, frailty, and brain diseases like Alzheimer's. As we get older, our ability to manage inflammation decreases. This creates a downward spiral—aging increases inflammation, which accelerates aging and raises the risk of chronic disease.

It's important to remember that inflammation isn't the cause of disease; it's the effect of something else. Anti-inflammatory drugs might seem like a quick, easy fix to inflammation. However, they don't address the root causes of chronic inflammation. By understanding the root causes of chronic inflammation, we can take steps to counteract it and support proper immune function.

Actionable Steps for Reducing Inflammation

> He said, "If you will carefully obey the Lord your God, do
> what is right in his sight, pay attention to his commands, and
> keep all his statutes, I will not inflict any illnesses on you that I
> inflicted on the Egyptians. For I am the Lord who heals you."

(Exodus 15:26 *CSB*)

Each decision—what we eat, the products we use, and our daily activities—either fuels or fights inflammation. By making healthier choices, we can reclaim our health span and better honor our bodies as temples of the Holy Spirit.

Subsequent chapters will explore the multipronged approach to an anti-inflammatory lifestyle in depth. In the meantime, you can start today with these simple steps:

1. **Diet:** Introduce one new anti-inflammatory food into your diet this week—such as leafy greens, berries, fatty fish, nuts, or olive oil. At the same time, reduce processed foods, gluten, sugary items, and unhealthy fats (e.g., avoid fast food and skip processed items at the grocery store).

2. **Movement:** Aim for at least 30 minutes of moderate activity, like brisk walking or cycling, most days of the week. Incorporate strength training exercises, like squats or resistance band exercises, two to three times per week to build muscle and boost metabolism.

3. **Stress Reduction:** Start each day with a 5-minute deep breathing or meditation practice to cultivate calm and relaxation.

Don't let chronic inflammation hinder your ability to serve as a vessel for God's purposes. Your journey toward a life free from the grip of chronic inflammation begins today. Every small step you take can bring you closer to a vibrant, energetic, and fulfilling life.

Inflammation, Intervention, and Advocacy

In that moment, when my husband was wheeled back into the ER, I realized how fragile life could be, and how quickly everything could change.

The ER staff reversed my husband's morphine and gave him a double dose of Zofran for the nausea, despite my insistence that it wasn't working. After a battery of tests, he was admitted to the hospital, awaiting surgery and worsening by the hour.

Then a hospitalist appeared—a doctor I believe God sent. She truly listened as I explained that the morphine was causing his nausea and the Zofran wasn't working. I asked if she would switch his medications and suggested Toradol, an anti-inflammatory, to possibly reduce his need for opioids to manage pain. She agreed.

Within hours, things began to improve.

His nausea disappeared. His pain decreased (except his hunger pain). And for the first time in days, he could swallow his own saliva.

Later, the surgeon came in and admitted, "I'm afraid we did this to you." It was a bittersweet acknowledgment that their interventions had caused his suffering. He had deteriorated under their care, losing weight, strength, and cognitive function—all while still receiving no nutrition. I doubted he could survive any surgical complications in his condition.

I strongly advocated for total parenteral nutrition (TPN), a method of delivering essential nutrients intravenously. Though hesitant, the surgeon eventually agreed. She explained they typically needed to justify the high cost of TPN by keeping it in place for at least two weeks.

Within 24 hours on TPN, my husband dramatically improved—walking, talking, and even joking again. We managed to move his surgery up by switching to a more senior surgeon.

A Crisis That Could Have Been Avoided

Chronic inflammation is often called a silent killer because it quietly erodes health until crisis strikes. For my husband, it became his body's greatest enemy.

This harrowing experience taught me three valuable lessons:

1. Both unchecked inflammation and medical errors can have devastating consequences.

2. Proper nutrition is not optional—when it's ignored, the consequences can be life-threatening.

3. In a system that often prioritizes costs over care, we must be relentless advocates for ourselves and those we love.

I thank God for His providence and the hospitalist for stepping in with anti-inflammatory medication when my husband needed it most. But as I reflected on the ordeal, I couldn't help but wonder: Could early intervention with anti-inflammatory strategies have prevented this crisis in the first place?

Toradol had worked so quickly. The relief was almost immediate, and I couldn't help but think—of course inflammation was involved! If his esophagus was constricted, of course it was inflamed. And if achalasia is an autoimmune disease, of course inflammation played a role. Why didn't the doctors consider that? Why did I have to request the Toradol?

Then it hit me—they didn't think about it because they don't yet understand achalasia as an autoimmune disease, or how inflammation drives autoimmunity in the first place. *Good grief.* The pieces fit together so clearly, yet the medical system was still operating as if they didn't.

Surgery was necessary, but even afterwards, we had to focus on reducing inflammation to support his recovery. That's what changed my perspective forever: Instead of waiting for a crisis, what if we focused on prevention before the damage begins?

What steps will you take today to prevent or break the cycle of chronic inflammation in your body?

PART THREE

Living Out God's Prescription

INTRODUCTION
TO PART THREE

Know Better, Do Better

*"Do the best you can until you know better.
Then when you know better, do better."*

—Maya Angelou

Congratulations on making it this far. You've taken in a lot of information—perhaps more than you expected—but I hope you've also started implementing small steps to lay the foundation for meaningful change. In this section, my goal is to help you build on that foundation, one step at a time, without feeling overwhelmed.

Trying to do everything at once can lead to burnout, but steady progress allows you to build momentum and confidence. Scripture echoes this wisdom in Proverbs 6:6 (CSB), reminding us to *"Go to the ant, you slacker; Observe its ways and be wise!"* Just as the ant steadily works toward its goal, small, intentional steps taken consistently lead to lasting transformation.

Those I know living a "clean" lifestyle didn't do it overnight. There will be things you cling to more tightly than others, but if you listen to God's prompting, He will gently guide you toward change.

For example, I've always found tea comforting and was reluctant to give it up. When I learned that tannins in tea can interfere with iron absorption, I cut back on black tea and saw improvements in my ferritin levels. Later, I discovered caffeine can irritate the bladder, so I limited my intake to one caffeinated cup in the morning. More recently, I realized that many companies spray their tea bags with plastic or use plastic to attach the string. This led me to seek compostable bags with tied strings and to drink more herbal and loose-leaf teas.

Embracing a healthier lifestyle is a journey, and discipline plays a crucial role. But discipline is not restriction—it's freedom. Someone who kicks the junk food habit is free from its grip. A smoker who quits gains freedom to breathe deeply again. True self-control isn't about missing out; it's about reclaiming your health, energy, and ability to serve others with joy and purpose.

Living out *God's Prescription* requires more than willpower; it requires His strength. As Zechariah 4:6 (*NIV*) says, *"Not by might nor by power, but by my Spirit."* True transformation happens when we surrender to God, embrace discipline, and take responsibility for our choices.

> *But be doers of the word and not*
> *hearers only, deceiving yourselves.*
>
> (James 1:22 *CSB*)

You've learned the principles—now it's time to put them into action. Knowledge alone won't change your life; action will. Yet studies show that many people resist change, even when facing a life-threatening illness. Will you defy the odds?

CHAPTER 10

The Myth of the Perfect Diet: Embracing a Flexible Approach

God also said, "Look, I have given you every seed-bearing plant on the surface of the entire earth and every tree whose fruit contains seed. This food will be for you."

(Genesis 1:29 CSB)

Before I knew better, I followed all the 'reputable' health advice: low-fat everything, margarine, skim milk, and diet soda. I thought I was making healthy choices and could exercise away dietary missteps, but I was setting myself up for trouble. Over time, my gut and brain couldn't handle the artificial sweeteners, carbonation, and chemicals. I see this with my clients—well-meaning people following the rules, only to end up exhausted, inflamed, confused, and discouraged.

Researchers found 71% of Americans rate their diet as good, very good, or excellent. Yet 70% scored an "F" for dietary quality based on dietary recalls and objective scoring. Rising rates of obesity, diabetes, and chronic illness support these findings.

We're told to consult doctors about dietary changes, yet most physicians receive minimal nutrition training, leading to gaps in dietary advice. At the same time, both professionals and the public often latch onto one approach—ketogenic, vegan, fasting, or carnivore—convinced it's the universal solution, ignoring individual nutritional needs.

But what if we could honor God's provision of nourishing foods while adapting to individual needs and to seasons of life? What if there was a flexible framework combining timeless wisdom with modern nutritional science?

In my nutritional therapy training and master's program, I studied many diets, from Paleo-Mediterranean to vegan and more. One key takeaway that stood out: there is no one-size-fits-all diet. Health is about finding what works for your body in this season of life.

In this chapter, we'll explore a new way to nourish your body that is both satisfying and sustainable. This approach can help you regain your energy and feel your best. We'll begin with the foundation: stable blood sugar, also known as blood glucose, and build a flexible, personalized eating plan you can adapt for life.

The Blood Sugar Balancing Act

At the heart of every optimal diet—regardless of philosophy—is one universal principle: stable blood sugar. It's essential for sustained energy, mental clarity, and long-term health.

Your body is designed to maintain blood sugar within a narrow range. Spikes or crashes can leave you feeling tired, irritable, or unfocused. Over time, unstable blood sugar contributes to insulin resistance, weight gain, and inflammation. These lead to chronic conditions like diabetes, heart disease, and cognitive decline.

Balancing macronutrients—carbohydrates, protein, and fat—is key to regulating blood sugar. Each serves a unique purpose:

- **Carbohydrates** are like fast-burning kindling. They provide quick energy but cause sharp spikes and drops in your energy levels if you eat them alone.

- **Protein** acts as medium-sized logs, delivering steady energy and moderating carbs' effects on blood sugar.
- **Fats** are like large, slow-burning logs that offer lasting fuel and keep blood sugar stable.

A common mistake is eating "naked" carbohydrates (e.g., plain toast or fruit) without protein, fiber, or fat to slow glucose absorption. This leads to spikes and crashes, leaving you tired and craving more sugar or reaching for caffeine.

As a child, I noticed this effect firsthand and told my mother I needed sausage with my pancakes to avoid being hungry by ten o'clock. Even now, starting the day with naked carbs leaves me hungrier than fasting does.

Macronutrient Ratios

Finding the right ratio of macronutrients to balance blood sugar takes some experimentation. The right ratios are widely debated, but there is no universal right answer. What works for one person may not work for another. However, diets high in carbohydrates— especially refined carbs in processed foods—cause blood sugar spikes and crashes.

Using a Continuous Glucose Monitor to Personalize Your Diet

A continuous glucose monitor (CGM) gives you real-time information about how your body reacts to different foods and meals. Even for non-diabetics, it can help identify patterns and highlight foods that cause blood sugar spikes or crashes.

With a family history of diabetes, I've always been mindful of my blood sugar. Since childhood, I've experienced feeling "hangry" when I skipped meals. In my 20s, I learned that while it wasn't hypoglycemia, my blood sugar could plummet. Wearing a CGM recently confirmed that this pattern persists for me. Being more aware of this has helped me focus on slow-burning fats and proteins, and better meal timing for glucose stability.

Stable blood sugar is essential for optimal health. I encourage you to experiment with macronutrient ratios and consider using a CGM. Other ways to stabilize your blood sugar are to exercise regularly, get sufficient sleep, manage your stress, and let your body guide you toward what works best.

Food as Medicine: A Framework for Whole-Body Health

Many clients come to me frustrated, feeling like food has become their enemy. They struggle with gut issues, low energy, and brain fog, often leaving doctors' offices with only a prescription—often an antidepressant—and no real answers.

To identify their triggers and begin healing, clients start on a tailored elimination diet. This helps calm the immune system and support healing, but elimination diets aren't intended for long-term use. That's why I developed the Anti-Inflammatory Rainbow Diet (AIRD)—a sustainable, adaptable framework designed to reduce inflammation, the root of chronic disease, and promote whole-body health. AIRD combines the wisdom of traditional diets with modern nutritional science, offering a practical starting point to improve and maintain health through life's seasons.

Anti-Inflammatory Rainbow Diet: A Whole-Food Approach

"What's on the end of your fork either feeds health or disease."

—Author Unknown

The AIRD is more than a diet—it's a lifestyle focused on nourishing and restoring your body. Emphasizing colorful, whole foods supports balanced blood sugar and gut health with prebiotic fiber. It also supports a healthy acid-alkaline balance, with animal foods consumed in moderation.

As we explore the AIRD framework, it's worth reflecting on Scripture:

Can't you see that the food you put into your body cannot defile you? Food doesn't go into your heart, but only passes through the stomach and then goes into the sewer. (By saying this, he declared that every kind of food is acceptable in God's eyes.) And then, he added, "It is what comes from inside that defiles you."

(Mark 7:18-20 *NLT*)

"Everything is permissible for me,"
but not everything is beneficial.

(1 Corinthians 6:12 *CSB*)

In declaring all foods clean, Jesus wasn't giving a free pass to consume anything without thought. Instead, He revealed a deeper truth: defilement comes from within—from our thoughts, words, and actions—not from what we eat. While all foods are spiritually clean, many modern food-like products no longer resemble the nourishing foods God created.

Modern Food Realities

Consider wheat. In biblical times, it was a simple, nutrient-dense grain. Leavened bread was fermented for easier digestion. Today's wheat varieties are hybridized or genetically modified, with proteins far different from what Jesus ate. Additionally, wheat is frequently treated with glyphosate to aid drying. Similarly, modern dairy comes from crossbred cows raised on unnatural diets, resulting in milk with more allergenic proteins. Ultra-pasteurization destroys beneficial enzymes.

Soy, often marketed as healthy, is typically genetically modified, sprayed with glyphosate, and heavily processed. Even wine differs dramatically from biblical times. Commercial production typically involves genetically modified yeast and sulfite preservatives, with higher alcohol and sugar content.

When you add processed sugars, industrial seed oils, factory-farmed meats, and commercial dairy, it's clear that much of today's food strays far from God's original design for nourishment.

This chapter isn't about legalism or rigid rules; it's about making informed choices that honor God's design for our bodies. As Hippocrates said, "Let food be thy medicine and medicine be thy food," reminding us that God provided healing foods to nourish and restore us. The foods I encourage you to avoid—processed foods, gluten, dairy, soy, sugar, GMOs, and seed oils—aren't spiritually 'unclean' but have been altered in ways that harm our health.

Eat This, Not That: Making Healthier Choices

"Nothing looks or tastes as good as being healthy feels."

—Author Unknown

Years ago, I attended a medical training where the consensus was clear: If every patient or client eliminated gluten, dairy, soy, and sugar, their health would improve dramatically. Similarly, at a functional medicine conference, practitioners agreed that avoiding GMOs led to major health benefits. These ideas are the foundation of AIRD. It focuses on avoiding inflammatory foods and embracing nutrient-rich alternatives.

It's not just gluten in wheat that can be problematic. Components like wheat germ agglutinin (WGA), a lectin found in the germ tissue of wheat kernels, can trigger immune responses and increase intestinal permeability. Modern processing methods often fail to neutralize these compounds, making them more likely to cause harm.

Avoiding processed foods is a cornerstone of any healthy diet. AIRD takes it further by identifying specific whole foods that can still be reactive, inflammatory, or harmful. Some recommendations, like giving up long-loved staples, may feel controversial or even sacrilegious. However, they're grounded in science and designed to help you thrive. *The Smart Food Swaps* table offers practical alternatives to get you started.

Want an easy way to remember the foods to avoid? Check the Resources for a downloadable card.

Smart Food Swaps	
Avoid	**Choose**
Gluten	Naturally gluten-free whole grains: quinoa, amaranth, teff, millet, various colors of rice (black, brown, red), oats (processed in a gluten-free facility), wild rice.
Commercial dairy	Non-dairy options: coconut or various nut milks and yogurt, or make your own (see Resources section).
Sugar	Natural sweeteners in moderation: dates, honey, maple syrup.
Soy	Chickpea-based miso, coconut aminos, or No Soy Tamari (see Resources section).
GMO Foods	Organic or non-GMO certified options.
Seed oils, hydrogenated, and partially hydrogenated oils	Healthy fats: olive oil, avocado oil, grass-fed butter or ghee.
© 2025 Terri Ward	

The Rainbow of Health: Phytonutrients and Color

The AIRD is named for the vibrant array of colors in fruits and vegetables. Each color represents unique phytonutrients and polyphenols that support health. These natural plant compounds act as antioxidants, reduce inflammation, and protect against chronic diseases. Polyphenols, in particular, help combat oxidative stress and promote overall well-being.

Eating a colorful variety of fruits and vegetables ensures a wide range of phytonutrients, which helps prevent deficiencies and disease. Mixing and matching colors on your plate maximizes these benefits. My husband often jokes, "I really scored points with this colorful meal!" Here are just a few examples of phytonutrients by color and their health benefits:

- **Red:** Lycopene lowers the risk of breast cancer and type 2 diabetes (T2DM).
- **Orange:** Beta-carotene reduces the risk of diabetes and death from all causes, including cardiovascular disease.
- **Yellow:** Alpha-carotene cuts the risk of certain cancers and all-cause mortality; lutein lowers diabetes risk; lutein combined with zeaxanthin reduces bladder and breast cancer risk.
- **Green:** Lutein lowers T2DM risk; chlorophyll alleviates seasonal allergies and supports weight loss.
- **Blue/Purple:** Anthocyanins combat inflammation and oxidative stress.
- **White:** Flavones lower the risk of certain cancers and all-cause mortality.

To make it easier to incorporate a colorful array of produce, the table, *A Rainbow of Fruits and Vegetables*, lists fruits and vegetables by color. Use it as a guide to 'eat the rainbow' and maximize the health benefits associated with each hue.

A Rainbow of Fruits and Vegetables		
Color	**Fruits**	**Vegetables**
Red	Apple, blood orange, cherry, cranberry, currant, red dragon fruit, guava, pomegranate, prickly pear, red grape, strawberry, raspberry, tomato, watermelon.	Beet, radish, red bell pepper. chard, and onion. rhubarb.
Orange	Apricot, cantaloupe, golden kiwi, mandarin, mango, orange, papaya, persimmon, pumpkin, tangerine, pumpkin.	Carrot, orange cauliflower, squash (winter), sweet potato, yellow bell pepper,
Yellow	Banana, golden delicious apple, lemon, pineapple, starfruit, yellow fig, pear, tomato, and watermelon.	Golden beet, yellow bell pepper, carrot, and summer squash.
Green	Green apple and grape, honeydew melon, green fig, gooseberry, kiwi, lime.	Cruciferous: arugula, bok choy, broccoli, broccoli sprouts, Brussels sprouts, cabbage, collard greens, dandelion greens, kale, kohlrabi, mustard greens, Swiss chard, turnip greens, watercress. Other: asparagus, green bell pepper, celery, cucumber, fennel, leek, okra, pea, scallion, spinach, zucchini.
Blue/ Purple	Acia berry, blueberry, blackberry, chokecherry (aronia), elderberry, huckleberry, purple grape, plum.	Eggplant, purple asparagus, Belgian endive, cabbage, kale, and sweet potatoes.
White/ Tan	Asian pear, coconut, lychee, white mulberry and peach.	Cauliflower, celeriac, daikon radish, garlic, Jerusalem artichokes, jicama, mushrooms, onions, parsnips, turnips, white kohlrabi.
© 2025 Terri Ward		

With such a vibrant array of fruits and vegetables, there's no shortage of nourishing options to explore—many readily available in your local supermarket. Why not challenge yourself to try something new? And this is just the beginning. Let's dive into fat and protein options.

Healthy Fats and Quality Proteins: Building Blocks of Health

Fats and proteins aren't just fuel—they're essential for your body's foundation. Fats support brain function, build cell membranes, and provide lasting energy. Proteins drive digestion, immunity, and cellular repair, acting as the backbone for enzymes, hormones, and muscles. Together, they promote vitality, a feeling of fullness, and optimal health.

Healthy Fats

Not all fats are created equal. Refined oils are stripped of nutrients and may promote inflammation. Prioritize unrefined options that protect against oxidative stress and supply essential fatty acids. For best quality, choose oils in small, dark-colored glass bottles to prevent rancidity caused by light. For high-heat cooking, use ghee, coconut oil, palm oil, and animal fats. Here are some healthy fats:

- Organic butter and ghee (from grass-fed cows)
- Coconut oil (first cold-pressed)
- Sustainable palm oil (ethically sourced)
- Extra virgin avocado oil (for lower heat cooking than refined up to about 375°F)
- Extra virgin olive oil (use raw or for low-heat cooking)
- Flaxseed oil (always use raw and refrigerate)
- Nuts and seeds
- Duck fat, tallow, and lard (from naturally raised animals)

These fats don't just add flavor. They're also required for absorbing fat-soluble vitamins (A, D, E, and K).

Quality Proteins

Proteins are the building blocks of life, but quality matters. Conventionally raised animals are often given antibiotics and fed unnatural diets, such as GMO corn, resulting in lower nutrient density and higher inflammatory fat profiles. Choose naturally raised proteins for better nutrient and fat content and fewer toxins:

- Wild game
- Grass-fed and grass-finished beef
- Free-range poultry (raised without antibiotics or unnatural feeds)
- Wild-caught fatty fish (Atlantic or Pacific mackerel, salmon, trout, herring, sardines, anchovies)
- Legumes (soaked, drained, and pressure cooked)

While pork and seafood are no longer considered spiritually unclean for Christians (Mark 7:19), their inclusion in a healthy diet remains debated. As scavengers, these animals have historically posed risks of parasites. Today they can accumulate toxins like mercury and microplastics. If you choose to eat them, I recommend sourcing naturally raised or wild-caught options. For a deeper exploration, check out the Resources.

By choosing unrefined oils and naturally raised proteins, you're avoiding harmful compounds, maximizing nutrient density, and supporting your body's ability to thrive. These nutrient-dense choices, combined with a colorful variety of organic fruits and vegetables, create a solid foundation for vibrant health.

To put this all together, refer to the pictured AIRD place setting as your guide for building balanced, anti-inflammatory meals.

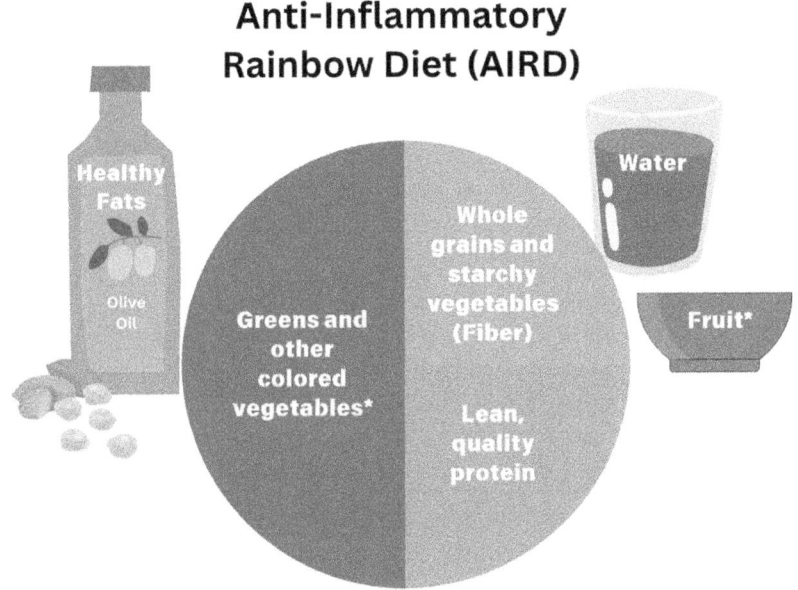

Anti-Inflammatory Rainbow Diet (AIRD)

Healthy Fats

Olive Oil

Greens and other colored vegetables*

Whole grains and starchy vegetables (Fiber)

Lean, quality protein

Water

Fruit*

Aim for variety, color, and balance with each meal.
*Include at least 1 serving per day each of *cruciferous vegetables* and *dark leafy greens;* limit fruit to 1-2 servings per day.

© 2025 Terri Ward

Spicing Up Health with Herbs and Spices

Long before pharmaceuticals, herbs and spices were valued for their healing properties. Today, they continue to provide health benefits and phytonutrients while enhancing meals. Encouraged by friends who loved my spice blends, I created Spice Cure, my spice blend company that offers healthy, allergy-friendly seasonings made with clean, organic ingredients as "The cure for boring food."

My blends include anti-inflammatory herbs and spices, such as basil, celery seed, chili powder, chives, cinnamon, marjoram, oregano, paprika, sage, and shallot. Other powerful options you might try are turmeric, ginger, rosemary, fennel seed, and anise seed. Try experimenting with different herbs and spices to transform ordinary dishes into flavorful, healthful meals.

Simple Steps to Living the Rainbow

The AIRD isn't about rigid rules, counting calories, or chasing numbers on a scale. It's about embracing colorful, whole foods that reduce inflammation and support your unique needs. It recognizes that health comes in all shapes and sizes.

AIRD's strength lies in its flexibility. Whether you want more balance, need to address health problems, or follow diets like low-FODMAP (Fermentable Oligosaccharides, Disaccharides, Monosaccharides, and Polyols) or AIP (autoimmune protocol), AIRD can help. With so many foods to choose from, you can easily adjust the macronutrient ratios or eliminate certain foods without feeling restricted. Plus, your taste preferences will evolve as your taste buds regenerate every 10 days, making it easier to adapt to new, nourishing foods.

Transitioning to an anti-inflammatory lifestyle may seem daunting. Remember that even minor changes can lead to significant improvements. The following steps will help you integrate the principles of AIRD and blood sugar balance into your daily life.

Practical Tips for Balancing Blood Sugar

1. Start meals with protein and fiber.
2. Avoid blue light exposure during meals (phones, tablets, TVs).
3. Use a CGM (see the Resources).
4. Fast for at least 12 hours overnight by avoiding food after dinner.

Simple Steps to Embrace AIRD

1. Eliminate processed foods and those listed in the Smart Food Swaps table earlier in the chapter.
2. Add more colorful foods to your plate.
3. Replace seed oils with healthy fats.

Kick It Up

Now that you're in the implementation phase of *God's Prescription*, it's time to build on the momentum from earlier chapters. Minor changes are powerful, but the more you commit, the more transformative your results will be.

Healing is a journey, not a race. You may notice improved energy, sharper thinking, better moods, and sounder sleep within weeks, but consistency is key. Progress matters more than perfection, so start where you are and keep moving forward. Remember, you're not alone; reach out for support if you need encouragement along the way.

Seasons of Health: Embracing God's Design

To everything there is a season, A time for every purpose under heaven.

(Ecclesiastes 3:1 *NKJV*)

This timeless truth applies not only to life's changes, but also to how we nourish our bodies. God, in His wisdom, provided healing foods to sustain us through every season of life. Just as the earth produces different foods in different seasons, our bodies have changing needs. As I reflect on my own journey from blindly following health trends to embracing my body's changing needs and the need for a personalized approach, I see how this wisdom can transform lives.

I see this transformation when I work with clients. They come seeking a clear plan, and I give them one—but more importantly they learn how to listen to their bodies. Instead of following rigid rules, they begin to understand what their body needs. Over time, they shift from seeking the "perfect" diet to learning how to make choices that align with both their needs and God's design for each season of life.

Healing often requires a comprehensive approach that combines personalized nutrition with medical interventions. Too often, people, including healthcare providers, resort to medications or procedures like surgery or injections before considering their diet, hoping for an easy fix. While the answer may be as simple as what's on their plate, healing often requires both medical interventions and lifestyle changes.

For instance, in situations like cancer treatment, diet is most effective when used alongside medical interventions, not as an afterthought. Just as we can't ignore winter's chill and expect spring blooms without preparation, lasting healing requires changing the internal environment that allows disease to thrive.

That's why AIRD, like the changing seasons, isn't a rigid plan but a flexible framework —one that adapts to your body's evolving needs. It prioritizes whole, unprocessed foods to stabilize blood sugar and support gut and immune health. Just as nature adjusts to each season, AIRD allows for adjustments based on individual health goals and seasons of life. As we adapt and make choices about our diet and lifestyle, we're called to remember:

> *So whether you eat or drink or whatever you do,*
> *do it all for the glory of God.*

(1 Corinthians 10:31 *NIV*)

As you reflect on your own health, consider this: What is your body asking for in this season? Have you been fighting against it, or are you ready to listen?

CHAPTER 11

Escaping Busyness: Prioritizing Time, Rest, and Renewal

"Time is what we want most, but what we use worst."

—William Penn

Years ago, I accompanied my dad to a cardiology appointment. Introducing me to his cardiologist, he said, "This is my daughter Terri. She used to be a CPA. I thought that was okay, but now she thinks she should tell people what they should and shouldn't eat."

That moment was both hurtful and eye-opening—not just because of his clear disapproval of my new profession, but because I had never realized he approved of my previous one.

I had spent years working long hours, sacrificing sleep and family time, and nearly destroying my health in the pursuit of success. In today's culture, workaholism is an acceptable addiction. We glorify busyness, overscheduling ourselves and our children, leaving no room for rest or reflection—no margin.

Even with the weight of His ministry and multitudes seeking Him, Jesus prioritized rest. He told His disciples, *"Come away by yourselves to a remote place and rest for a while."* (Mark 6:31 CSB). If the Son of God saw rest as essential, shouldn't we?

In our busyness, we often neglect essentials—time with God, nourishing food, restorative rest, and mindful movement. Everything seems important until we get sick, and then health becomes the priority.

This chapter is about creating sustainable rhythms and margin in our lives before burnout hits. We'll explore ways to balance stress, rest, and renewal through strategies like good sleep hygiene, joyful movement, nature and sound therapy, fasting, and heat/cold exposure. Finding balance isn't about doing more; it's about doing what matters most.

Making Room for What Matters Most

Pay careful attention, then, to how you walk—not as unwise people but as wise—making the most of the time, because the days are evil.

(Ephesians 5:15-16 *CSB*)

Doing what matters most requires intentionality—aligning our calendars with our priorities and purpose and shifting our focus from constant doing to intentional being.

Planning is essential at every stage of life—whether you're a student juggling assignments, a parent balancing work and family, or a retiree wondering how you ever had time to work. Without clear priorities, our schedules can quickly fill up with activities that leave us drained and unfulfilled.

Ask Yourself: Am I running my schedule, or is my schedule running me?

Creating an Ideal Calendar

Before you do anything, put your trust totally in God and not in yourself. Then every plan you make will succeed.

(Proverbs 16:3 *TPT*)

To take control of your calendar—rather than letting it control you—start by establishing clear priorities. Take time to pray and reflect on where you are and where you'd like to be in these areas of life:

- **Mental and Spiritual:** Prayer, Scripture, and personal growth.
- **Physical:** Exercise, nutrition, and mindfulness practices.
- **Financial:** Budgeting, stewardship, and planning.
- **Spouse:** Quality time and shared goals.
- **Family:** Time with children and extended family.
- **Community/Friends:** Church, meaningful connections, and service.
- **Personal/Margin:** Hobbies, rest, and downtime.
- **Work:** Aligning career goals with personal values and calling.

Once you've identified and updated your priorities, put them into action by creating an *Ideal Calendar* (see the Resources). My first coaches, Leslie Jones and Martin Kettlehut, taught me this life-changing exercise. Scheduling what's most important first ensures your priorities don't get crowded out by the urgent but less important.

> *Honor the Lord with your possessions and with the first produce of your entire harvest.*
>
> (Proverbs 3:9 CSB)

Instead of reaching for your phone when you wake up, prioritize God by giving Him the first moments of your day, inviting His guidance and blessing into everything that follows.

Connecting Scripture, Science, and Intentional Living

Both Scripture and science affirm the importance of intentional planning. *The plans of the diligent certainly lead to profit, but anyone who is reckless certainly becomes poor* (Proverbs 21:5 CSB). When our time, relationships, and health are in balance, we experience greater peace and fulfillment.

Research confirms that clear priorities and boundaries reduce stress and improve productivity. Time management is also correlated with life satisfaction and better mental health. Sustainable health requires balance. Without it, even the best health strategies won't be effective. True wellness is about how we steward our time, relationships, and God-given responsibilities.

Overcoming Resistance and Building Self-Discipline

We often resist what's good for us. As Counselor Patricia Cook, LMFT, said, "People choose familiar pain over the novel unknown." Growth lies beyond our comfort zones.

Many people sacrifice health for wealth, only to later spend their wealth trying to regain health. Prioritizing career over well-being can lead us to rely more on worldly success than God's provision. Time is more valuable than money. Investing it wisely today benefits future health. Wealth cannot buy back lost health.

Dr. Ben Lynch wisely said, "Health is a four-letter word spelled W-O-R-K." A popular saying goes, "We first make our habits, then our habits make us." Hebrews 12:11 (*CSB*) affirms the importance of self-discipline and perseverance: *"No discipline seems enjoyable at the time, but painful. Later on, however, it yields the peaceful fruit of righteousness to those who have been trained by it."*

Fasting is an effective way to cultivate self-discipline. It teaches us to resist immediate comfort for greater rewards—physically and spiritually. Let's explore how this ancient practice can help us reclaim health and refocus on what truly matters.

Fasting: Connecting Spiritual and Physical Benefits

Biblical fasting is a spiritual discipline involving abstaining from food (and sometimes drink) for a period of time. The primary purpose is to humble oneself before God, seek His will, and demonstrate dependence on Him rather than worldly sustenance. The Bible doesn't explicitly command fasting. We don't have to do it—just like we don't have to honor our temples. However, Jesus expected it. In Matthew 6:16-18, He didn't say, *if you fast*, but *"When you fast…"*

Modern science has uncovered profound physiological benefits of fasting, aligning with biblical wisdom:

- **Cellular Autophagy:** Fasting triggers autophagy, a process where cells remove damaged components and regenerate, like cleansing for the cells. (Psalm 51:10 *NIV– "Create in me a clean heart, O God, and renew a steadfast spirit within me."*)

- **Metabolic Benefits:** Fasting improves insulin sensitivity, promotes fat loss, and supports metabolic health as well as the gut microbiota. (Proverbs 25:28 *NIV– "Like a city whose walls are broken through is a person who lacks self-control."*)

- **Cognitive Clarity:** Fasting enhances mental clarity and brain function, giving us greater wisdom. (Daniel 9:3 *NIV– "So I turned to the Lord God and pleaded with him in prayer and petition, in fasting, and in sackcloth and ashes."*)

- **Reduced Inflammation:** Studies show that fasting lowers inflammation and oxidative stress, to help us heal. (Isaiah 58:6,8 *NIV– "Is not this the kind of fasting I have chosen: to loose the chains of injustice and untie the cords of the yoke, to set the oppressed free and break every yoke? Then your light will break forth like the dawn, and your healing will come quickly."*)

- **Longevity and Disease Prevention:** Research suggests fasting promotes longevity and may help prevent chronic diseases. (Proverbs 3:1-2 *NIV– "My son, do not forget my teaching, but* *keep my commands in your heart, for they will prolong your life many years and bring you peace and prosperity.")*

Scripture shows various fasting practices, from one-day fasts to extended 40-day periods, reflecting the flexibility and intentionality required.

Safe, Effective Intermittent Fasting for Today's World

For years, we've been told that small, frequent meals are best, that breakfast is the most important meal of the day, and that weight loss simply requires eating less and exercising more. But what if we've been looking at it all wrong? What if when we eat is just as important as, if not more than, what we eat?

When we graze throughout the day, we keep insulin levels elevated and rely solely on quick-burning sugar for fuel. This wreaks havoc on blood sugar levels, promotes oxidative stress, and drives inflammation. Intermittent fasting allows the body to tap into stored fat for sustained energy and metabolic efficiency.

Start with a 12-hour overnight fast, increasing by an hour every day or two, until you're fasting for 17 hours. Consume only water, coffee, or tea during the fasting period. It may take several weeks to experience the full effects, so don't give up too soon.

While many people report benefits from extended fasts of 24 hours or longer, they are not for everyone and should be approached cautiously under professional supervision.

Who Should Avoid Fasting?

- Children, adolescents, or seniors over 70
- Women who are pregnant, breastfeeding, or trying to conceive
- Individuals with diabetes, heart or kidney issues, or a history of eating disorders

Recommendations for women of menstruating age:

- Avoid fasting during ovulation (two weeks before your period).
- Avoid or limit fasting to 12 hours the week before menstruation.

Postmenopausal women may benefit from following a weekly cycle with five days of fasting.

Before beginning any fasting regimen, consult your healthcare provider, especially if you have underlying health conditions.

Fasting requires no special equipment or expensive supplements and can even save money on food while improving health and longevity. In fact, some of the best medicine comes at no cost at all.

Some of the Best Medicine Is Free

Many people spend money on cosmetic procedures, designer clothes, and entertainment, yet hesitate to invest in their health. The truth is: some of the most powerful healing tools are free.

The strategies below are supported by science and align with how God designed our bodies to heal and thrive.

Nature-Connecting Practices

Forest-bathing: Growing up in a small Montana town surrounded by mountains, I found that time spent in the forest brought a unique calmness and renewal. Science now confirms that spending time in nature offers measurable health benefits.

The Japanese practice of shinrin-yoku (forest bathing) is recognized worldwide for its restorative effects. Trees release phytoncides, which boost the immune system and encourage relaxation. Immersing yourself in forest sights, sounds, and scents can reduce stress, improve mood, sharpen our cognition, and lower cortisol levels, heart rates, and blood pressure.

God created nature not just for beauty, but for healing. As Psalm 23:2 (NIV) reminds us, *"He makes me lie down in green pastures; He leads me beside quiet waters."* Walking among trees and reconnecting with the natural world can restore balance and well-being.

Grounding (aka Earthing): Have you ever felt an unexplainable pull to the outdoors? That longing is more than a craving for fresh air—it's a reminder of our connection to God's creation. *"And the Lord God formed man of the dust of the ground"* (Genesis 2:7 *NKJV*), and science confirms our health is tied to the Earth.

Grounding involves making direct contact with the Earth's surface—walking barefoot on grass, sand, or soil. This allows our bodies to absorb the Earth's natural electrical charge, making it an effective strategy against inflammation, poor sleep, chronic stress, pain, and other conditions.

When Moses encountered God in the burning bush, he was told, *"Take off your sandals, for the place where you are standing is holy ground"* (Exodus 3:5 *NIV*). While this instruction was specific to that sacred moment, Psalm 24:1 reminds us, *"The earth is the Lord's."* Perhaps removing our shoes is more than a physical act—it's a way to reconnect with both creation and the Creator.

Even in the winter or when outdoor grounding isn't possible, grounding mats and sheets offer an effective, though not free, alternative to connect with the Earth's charge (see the Resources online).

Sunlight exposure: For those in gray-sky regions, a sun lamp can help boost mood, but nothing compares to natural sunlight. Regular exposure helps regulate our internal clock, supports vitamin D production, and boosts energy levels. Whether it's a morning walk or a few minutes on your porch, soaking up natural light is a simple way to recharge and restore balance.

Restorative Practices

Meditation: Christians often misunderstand meditation. Christian meditation is not about emptying the mind but focusing it—on Scripture, gratitude, or being present with God. Psalm 1:2 reminds us of meditating on God's Word. Christian meditation offers scientifically recognized benefits like reduced stress, improved focus, and emotional balance—while keeping our hearts fixed on God.

Sleep: My husband's doctor, in her thick Indian accent, once told him he needed better sleep "hahjeen." He had no idea she meant "hygiene" or what that was. I've emphasized the importance of sleep and its connection to health throughout this book. However, I haven't explained how to improve your sleep so you can heal and recharge. Sleep hygiene—healthy habits that support restful sleep—are the how.

Below are some simple sleep hygiene tips:

1. **Get natural light exposure:** Sunlight, particularly in the morning, helps regulate your body's circadian rhythms, promoting production of serotonin during the day and melatonin at night. This natural cycle supports deeper, more restful sleep. Aim for at least 15 to 30 minutes of morning sunlight.

2. **Exercise regularly:** Avoid exercising within three hours of bedtime.

3. **Limit naps:** If you must nap, keep it under 20 minutes to avoid disrupting nighttime sleep.

4. **Establish a bedtime routine:** A warm bath, journaling, or light stretching can help your body unwind.

5. **Maintain sleep and wake times:** These shouldn't deviate by more than 1 hour, even on weekends.

6. **Be in bed by 10 PM:** Every hour of sleep before midnight is more restorative than sleep after midnight due to our circadian rhythms.

7. **Optimize your sleep environment:** Keep your bedroom between 60 and 67°F, dark, and quiet. Use blackout curtains, turn clocks away from your view, and minimize electronic devices to reduce disruptive electromagnetic fields (EMFs).

8. **Minimize blue light exposure:** Blue light from electronic screens interferes with melatonin production. Reduce screen time before bed or wear blue-blocking glasses.

9. **Avoid caffeine, alcohol, and late-night eating:** Caffeine and alcohol can disrupt sleep quality. Finish eating before 8 PM to prevent digestive disruptions and support restful sleep.

Laughter: *A joyful heart is good medicine.* (Proverbs 17:22 *CSB*). Laughter releases endorphins, reduces stress, and promotes a sense of well-being. It can also improve circulation, boost the immune system, and even enhance pain tolerance.

Never underestimate the power of a good belly laugh. It's a simple, free, and effective way to restore balance and resilience. Whether through funny movies, jokes with friends, or laughter yoga, find ways to incorporate joy into your day.

Sound Therapy: Sound has long been a healing tool. Biblical references like David's harp soothing King Saul show music's emotional power. Research confirms music can reduce anxiety, respiration rate, blood pressure, and pain perception. Simple practices like listening to calming music, worshiping, or using instruments like singing bowls or tuning forks can restore balance and joy.

Sex: It's not just about physical pleasure or procreation. It counts as a form of moderate physical activity, supporting both physical and emotional health. Regular sexual activity has been shown to improve heart health, reduce stress, and promote better sleep. For men, it is associated with a lower risk of prostate cancer and may contribute to a longer lifespan.

Sex triggers the release of the feel-good hormones endorphins and oxytocin, which enhance happiness, strengthen emotional connection, and may even reduce pain. Within the covenant of marriage, sex is a gift that aligns with God's desire for us to experience joy and connection.

Other Practices: Of course, prayer is a must, but other practices that are free and require minimal time and effort include guided imagery, progressive muscle relaxation, and deep breathing exercises. Pick what works for you and practice it consistently.

Resilience-Building Practices

Movement: Some of the many benefits of exercise have been covered in previous chapters, including brain-derived neurotrophic factor (BDNF), which helps improve cognition, mood, and brain function. Just one workout can increase BDNF.

A study of men and women over 50 found that 16 weeks of aerobic exercise three times a week was as effective as an antidepressant in treating depression. Participants engaged in a warm-up, 30 minutes of brisk walking or jogging at a moderate-to-vigorous intensity, and a cool-down.

Exercise also causes your body to produce endorphins, boosting happiness and reducing stress perception. Find something enjoyable so you'll stick with it. Whether you hire a personal trainer, join a fitness class, or simply walk in nature – just move!

Heat and Cold Therapies: Psalm 147:17-18 (*NIV*) highlights God's design for cycles of warmth and cold: "He hurls down his hail like pebbles. Who can withstand his icy blast? He sends his word and melts them; he stirs up his breezes, and the waters flow."

- **Heat Therapy (aka hyperthermia):** Warm baths or heat packs relax muscles, improve circulation, and alleviate chronic pain.

175

Repeat exposure such as through hot baths or saunas increases BDNF. For those with access, saunas may also extend your health span and decrease your risk of dementia and Alzheimer's disease.

- **Cold Therapy:** Finishing showers with 30 to 90 seconds of cold water can reduce inflammation, enhance recovery, and improve mental resilience. Other forms of cold exposure, such as polar plunges, cold water immersion, and whole-body cryotherapy, offer similar benefits, including boosted circulation, reduced muscle soreness, and improved immune function. Start with shorter showers and gradually increase exposure as you adapt.

True wellness doesn't have to come with a hefty price tag. Simple, natural habits can deliver profound health benefits without straining your finances.

Small Steps to Big Change

> *Do not despise these small beginnings,*
> *for the Lord rejoices to see the work begin.*
>
> (Zechariah 4:10 *NLT*)

Lasting rest and renewal come through small, intentional changes practiced consistently. Instead of overhauling your entire routine at once, focus on one step at a time. Start with your calendar by prioritizing what truly matters. Then incorporate one new habit—whether grounding, laughter, or improved sleep hygiene. Each step builds a foundation for a healthier, more balanced life.

1. Create your *Ideal Calendar.*
2. Start each day with intention.
3. Say "No" to something unimportant this week.

4. Improve your sleep environment.

5. Commit to one of the free practices you've never tried before.

6. Reflect and adjust at the end of the week.

Bringing It All Together: Freedom, Responsibility, and Influence

When my dad said it wasn't right that I told people what they should and shouldn't eat, I replied, "God gave us free choice, and you can eat whatever you want." The nurse chimed in and said, "Yeah. It's better for business." We both snickered. Dad grunted.

We all have been given free choice. We don't "have" to do anything. Free thinking isn't holding firm to beliefs but having the courage to adjust them when presented with new truth. Just as we grow in faith, we must reevaluate our health choices based on new knowledge.

My dad smoked for decades and never wanted to quit. Then, after three hospital days without smoking, he decided not to restart. My mom struggled to quit for years until Dad quit. Their contrasting experiences showed me how difficult breaking unhealthy habits can be.

As I discussed in "The Average of 5" in chapter 1, our social circles significantly impact our health choices. While these circles shape us, the ultimate responsibility for our health lies in our own hands. Surrounding ourselves with people who prioritize health and intentional living can transform our journey.

It's easy to think health can be delayed, but our daily decisions determine our future health. While it's tempting to expect others to manage our health—whether healthcare providers or family members—ultimately, it's up to us.

Ask yourself: Am I truly taking responsibility for my health, or am I letting my habits control me?

CHAPTER 12

Sustainable Living: Managing Your Toxic Load

Although the Lord gives you the bread of adversity and the water of affliction, your teachers will be hidden no more; with your own eyes you will see them. Whether you turn to the right or to the left, your ears will hear a voice behind you, saying, "This is the way; walk in it."

(Isaiah 30:20-21 *NIV*)

About six years ago, we moved to Idaho and found a beautiful half-acre lot where we had our house built. After a few years, I began experiencing some health challenges. I struggled with energy and inflammation. I developed lichen sclerosus, an autoimmune condition, and my immune system started reacting to all kinds of different things. One reaction was severe enough to send me to the ER.

Then, I gained about 10 pounds for no reason and couldn't lose it. While I could have attributed these changes to aging, genetics, or bad luck, I knew better. I recalled from my environmental medicine class that toxins could contribute to excess weight, but thought I lived a pretty clean life. I searched for answers, considering several other possible causes, but when my body odor changed suddenly, I knew I was toxic.

Again, I could have ignored the signs and used a heavy-duty antiperspirant, but I believe that if you listen to your body's whispers, you won't have to listen to it scream. Think of it like what my dad called "idiot lights" on the dashboard of your vehicle. It's not wise to ignore those either.

I decided to get to the bottom of this quickly. I had testing done for mycotoxins, organic acids, glyphosate, heavy metals, and metabolites of various toxic chemicals. Thank God I decided to investigate! When my results were complete, the doctor from the lab called to ask if he could use my results for a presentation because I had so many elevated results!

Designed to Adapt, but Not Without Limits

This experience has deepened my understanding of how toxins affect our bodies. My former mentor, Dr. George Birnbach, once told me, "The human body wasn't designed to be healthy; it was designed to adapt." While our bodies are remarkably adept at adapting and detoxifying, this ability has its limits.

Genetics, diet, and lifestyle all influence how efficiently we process toxins. Some people seem to handle toxic exposures with ease. They can smoke for decades without obvious harm or tolerate a root canal without immune overload. Others, however, experience severe reactions to the same exposures.

Think of it as each of us having a "toxic bucket" of varying sizes, and various toxins help fill it. As long as the bucket doesn't overflow like mine did, we're fine. However, a little of too many things or adding a lot of one thing can overflow the bucket, leading to toxicity and disease. This concept aligns with a key principle in toxicology: "The dose makes the poison."

While God's blueprint for the human body is flawless, our world has become a toxic soup exposing us to harmful substances—even before birth. Researchers have found that the average placenta contains nearly 300 toxins! Sometimes things go awry during fetal development, contributing to lifelong health challenges, or worse.

Ultimately, chronic disease results from the body either lacking what it needs or being burdened by something harmful. But there's good news! When we give the body the right tools and remove harmful exposures, it has an incredible capacity to heal. God's design is miraculous—we just need to stop disrupting it.

Health Effects of Toxins

There is a way that seems right to a person,
but its end is the way to death.

(Proverbs 14:12 *CSB*)

With over 86,000 chemicals registered by the EPA, navigating potential health risks can feel overwhelming. While some countries require proof of safety before allowing chemicals in food and the environment, the U.S. often permits them until harm is proven—sometimes taking years. Despite growing evidence, many harmful chemicals persist in our daily lives.

Consider cosmetics and personal care products (PCPs) like shampoo, lotions, and fragrances. On average, an American woman uses 12 PCPs in her daily routine, introducing 168 different chemicals to her body. While men may use fewer products, their products also contain harmful substances. Common toxic ingredients in PCPs include:

- Parabens
- Phthalates

- Cyclosiloxanes
- Formaldehyde releasers
- Solvents
- Preservatives

Inadvertent contaminants with potentially carcinogenic chemicals like 1,4-dioxane may occur during manufacturing. Additionally, ingredients labeled as 'fragrances' are not required to be disclosed, making it difficult to know exactly what you're being exposed to.

In the EU, over 1,300 chemicals have been banned from cosmetics, but only 11 in the United States. These chemicals can be carcinogens, endocrine disrupting chemicals (EDCs), allergens, and inflammatory agents. In 2016, the FDA banned triclosan, an antibacterial agent, from hand soaps due to safety concerns. Studies show that triclosan is an EDC, potentially interfering with thyroid and other hormones. However, it is still allowed in toothpastes, cosmetics, deodorants, and other PCPs.

EDCs are substances that interfere with hormones produced by the body's endocrine glands, which regulate a wide range of vital functions. Hormones regulate more than just sex and thyroid function—they also control metabolism, stress response, blood sugar levels, growth, and development. When EDCs disrupt the endocrine system, they can contribute to health issues ranging from hormonal imbalances to chronic diseases and, in severe cases, even life-threatening conditions.

While exposure can be harmful for all ages, the stages from fetal development through adolescence may be more vulnerable. EDCs are linked to:

- Earlier puberty in girls
- Enlarged breasts in males (gynecomastia)
- Infertility in both sexes

- Pregnancy complications
- Thyroid issues
- Respiratory problems
- Immune dysfunction
- Neurological and cognitive issues
- Metabolic dysfunction, including diabetes
- Cardiovascular disease
- Cancer

Common Sources of Endocrine Disruptors

EDCs aren't just in cosmetics and PCPs, they're pervasive in our environment. The CDC estimates that 96% of Americans have bisphenol-A (BPA) in their blood. Listed below are some EDCs and their common sources:

Industrial Chemicals

- **Bisphenols:** Plastic food containers, water bottles, canned foods, receipts, dust.
- **Phthalates:** Plastic products, children's products, medical tubing, air near production facilities.
- **PCBs (polychlorinated biphenyls):** Industrial waste, contaminated soil and water, air near disposal sites.
- **PFAS (per- and polyfluoroalkyls):** Nonstick cookware, food packaging, clothing, drinking water.
- **Brominated flame retardants:** Furniture, fabrics, electronics, building materials, dust.
- **NPEs (Nonylphenol Ethoxylates):** Cleaning products, laundry detergents, water.

Pesticides and Agricultural Chemicals

- **Glyphosate:** Agricultural runoff, soil contamination, food residues, air, water.
- **Atrazine:** Herbicide in agricultural settings, water, soil.
- **2,4-D:** Widely used agricultural pesticide, air, water, soil.
- **Chlorpyrifos:** Agricultural and residential pesticide, food residues, air, water.
- **Vinclozolin:** Fungicide used in agriculture, food residues, soil.

Heavy Metals

- **Arsenic:** Rice, baby food, well water, soil.
- **Lead:** Municipal water, industrial exposure, dust, soil.
- **Cadmium:** Industrial sites, contaminated water, air, soil.
- **Mercury:** Fish and seafood, multi-dose vaccines, air, water.
- **Fluoride:** Fluoridated drinking water, some dental products.

Household Chemicals

- **Chlorine:** Cleaning products, water treatment, air.
- **Ammonia:** Cleaning and disinfecting products, air.
- **Perfluorinated compounds:** Stain-resistant fabrics, cookware, water, dust.

Toxins and toxicants are ubiquitous in our environment, leaving residues in our air, water, dust, and food. These substances—including pesticides, industrial compounds, flame retardants, pharmaceuticals, and heavy metals—create multiple pathways for ongoing exposure. They're inside us, on items we use daily, and all around us in our homes and workplaces.

Even microplastics (tiny plastic particles less than 5mm in size) have been found in human tissues, including the brain. While toxins are naturally occurring and toxicants are man-made, for simplicity, I'll refer to both as toxins.

Forever Chemicals

Not all toxins are easily eliminated from our bodies. Certain pesticides and medications can be processed and excreted fairly quickly, if our bodies function optimally. Thousands of others are more persistent. These 'forever chemicals', such as PCBs and PFAS, can linger in our tissues, including our brains, for years or even decades. These man-made substances also contaminate our soil, air, and food chain.

While this chapter highlights many common toxins, countless others exist in our environment. Understanding their effects is just the first step. We must also take action to reduce exposure and prevent our buckets from overflowing. As Fran Drescher, comedian and author of *Cancer Schmancer*, advises, think "In, On, and Around You."

Simple Swaps to Reduce Your Toxic Load

By following the AIRD, you're already avoiding many common toxins found in processed foods, conventionally raised meats, and non-organic produce. Making simple swaps in your home and personal care routine can further reduce your toxic burden. The table titled *Simple Swaps to Reduce Your Toxic Load* provides a list of practical alternatives.

While some options like water filtration can be costly, reducing your toxic load isn't always expensive. Using vinegar for cleaning, reusable wool dryer balls instead of dryer sheets, and choosing whole foods over processed options, are budget-friendly. It's all about making informed choices within your means.

185

Simple Swaps to Reduce Your Toxic Load	
Swap This	**For This**
Air fresheners	Air purifiers, essential oil diffusers
Plastic food containers	Glass or stainless with lids
Plastic wrap	Beeswax wraps
Plastic bags	PFAS-free silicone bags
Plastic cutting boards	Wood or tempered glass
Teflon/nonstick or aluminum cookware	Stainless steel, cast iron (tested for lead), safer nonstick options free of PFOA (perfluoroococtanoic acid) and PFOS (perfluororooctane sulfonate)
Aluminum foil	Parchment paper, lids
Chemical pesticides	Organic produce, natural pest control (e.g. diatomaceous earth, essential oil-based repellents)
High-mercury fish (tuna, swordfish)	Salmon, sardines, light tuna instead of albacore
Chemical cleaning products	Vinegar, baking soda, Castile soap, natural essential oils, silicone or wool dryer balls
Synthetic or treated fabrics	Organic cotton and PFAS-free fabrics, wet cleaning, liquid CO2, or silicone-based dry cleaning methods
Chemical-laden personal care products	Natural products free of parabens, phthalates, and synthetic fragrances, aluminum-free deodorant, mineral-based sunscreen
© 2025 Terri Ward	

Be sure to check out the Resources for this chapter. There, you'll find links to safer options, including swaps I've made and apps to check ingredients in foods and personal care products. You can also access recipes for making your own non-toxic personal care and cleaning products, as well as information on water testing and filtration systems.

Reducing exposure is a crucial step, but what about the toxins already in your body?

Detoxification: Supporting Your Body Safely

Therapeutic detoxification involves a complex process called "provocation," where toxins are deliberately mobilized from tissues and then eliminated. This is not something you should do on your own. When your body breaks down toxins, it transforms them into substances that can actually be more harmful. If your elimination pathways aren't clear they won't be eliminated and could make you feel worse or harm you.

Professional guidance should ensure detoxification is personalized. It should address specific areas and body systems where more support may be needed. It should also ensure all the necessary nutrients for the process are onboard and the right binders for targeted toxins are used. Most binders will also bind important nutrients, so caution is required.

Our body's main elimination pathways include urine, stool, bile, and sweat, and even breast milk can be a route for excretion. Signs such as lack of sweating or less than daily bowel movements may indicate impaired detoxification.

Removing heavy metals, especially mercury, requires professional intervention. Just as special care is needed when removing mercury dental fillings, eliminating it from your body demands specific chelating agents. Many of these agents are prescription-only and should only be used under medical supervision due to their potency and potential side effects.

Safe Support for Natural Detoxification

While the AIRD already provides a foundation, certain foods can further support your body's natural detoxification processes by enhancing liver function, digestion, and toxin elimination. Consider incorporating these foods into your daily meals to aid in gentle detoxification:

- **Sulfur-rich foods:** Cruciferous vegetables such as broccoli, cauliflower, and Brussels sprouts help boost detoxification enzymes in the liver.
- **Antioxidant-rich foods:** Berries, leafy greens, and colorful vegetables combat oxidative stress caused by toxins.
- **Fiber sources:** Oats, flax, chia seeds, and okra aid in binding and eliminating toxins through digestion.
- **Hydrating foods:** Cucumbers, watermelon, and citrus fruits, along with drinking plenty of clean water, support kidney function and toxin flushing.
- **Detoxifying herbs and spices:** Turmeric, ginger, and garlic have anti-inflammatory and liver-supportive properties.

Action Steps for Reducing Toxic Load

Incorporating stress management practices alongside the AIRD can also help reduce your toxic load. These additional strategies can further assist your body in eliminating toxins effectively:

1. **Hydration:** Staying well-hydrated is essential for flushing toxins through the kidneys. Aim to drink half your body weight (in pounds) in ounces of clean, filtered water daily. For example, if you weigh 150 pounds, drink at least 75 ounces per day—more if you're sweating or engaging in physical activity.

2. **Bowel Movements:** Regular elimination is crucial for detoxification. Ensure you're drinking enough water and consuming adequate fiber to support at least one healthy bowel movement per day.

3. **Sweat:** Exercise promotes circulation and supports detoxification by eliminating toxins through sweat. Incorporate activities that make you sweat regularly and consider using a sauna to further enhance this process.

4. **Read Labels:** Start reading labels on everything—from food to personal care products. The best foods, whole foods, don't have ingredient labels, but for those that do, understanding what's inside can help you make informed choices. Download apps that evaluate ingredients in foods and personal care items to guide your purchasing decisions (see the Resources).

5. **Reduce Exposure:** Prioritize the most significant sources of toxins "in, on, and around you." You don't need to discard everything immediately. Start by replacing products with healthier swaps as you run out of them or upgrade your home environment.

6. **Testing:** If you suspect your toxic burden is high, consider taking the Are You Toxic Quiz (see the Resources). Consult a functional medicine practitioner for testing. They can help assess your body's readiness for detoxification and guide you through safe, personalized protocols.

7. **Dry Brushing:** Dry brushing stimulates the lymphatic system, promoting circulation and detoxification. Before showering, use a natural bristle brush to gently sweep the skin in long, upward strokes toward the heart. Start at the feet and move upward to exfoliate and refresh the skin.

8. **Quality Sleep:** Your body detoxifies during sleep, clearing toxins from the brain. Seven to nine hours of high-quality sleep each night is optimal to support detoxification.

From Exposure to Empowerment

As I mentioned earlier, I had my own toxic wake-up call—an alarming phone call from the lab's doctor. That moment was my turning point.

My next mission was finding the sources of exposures because it makes no sense to try detoxifying if the source of exposure isn't eliminated. In chapter 7, I shared one source, which was a silent infection in my root canal. Another exposure came from black mold under the sink of the house we lived in while our house was being built. My mercury level was likely from the amalgam I had removed and/or the flu shots I got at the CPA firms where I worked decades ago.

Living near frequent aerial spraying by farmers and the county, I realized these practices may have added to my heavy metal burden. Pesticides and fertilizers often contain contaminants like lead, mercury, and cadmium, which drift far beyond fields, much like smoke from a fire. However, none of these potential sources explained why my uranium level was so high; I should have been glowing!

So, I had our well water tested, and it contained uranium, copper, and nitrates—contaminants that were silently building up inside me. Our well water tested at 43 micrograms per liter for uranium, exceeding the EPA's maximum contaminant level of 30!

Shortly after moving in, we installed a water softener and a reverse osmosis filtration system for our drinking water. However, for five years, I had been brushing my teeth, washing produce and dishes, watering the garden, and soaking in long baths. I had no idea I was being poisoned by our well water. I had trusted our builder and the water filter salesman when they said our water had been tested and was safe. However, it had never been tested for any of these substances.

I grew up in a small town where the city water was pure spring water that tasted much better than chlorinated city water. My grandparents had well water that tasted pure like ours, so I grew up thinking well water was good. Little did I know!

This experience taught me a crucial lesson:

But test everything that is said. Hold on to what is good.

(1 Thessalonians 5:21 *NLT*)

Learn from my mistake, and as President Reagan said, "Trust, but verify." Whether your water comes from a well or a municipal source, regular testing is essential. Different contaminants require different filtration methods, so stay informed and proactive. In our case, removing uranium required adding a whole-house anion exchange system after our water softener. This specialized system targets and removes negatively charged contaminants like uranium, arsenic, and nitrates.

Although my test results were concerning, they provided the clarity I needed to make meaningful changes. After installing a water filtration system and having my root canals extracted, I began a five-month detoxification protocol. By the time this book is published, I will have completed the protocol and retesting. Just a few months in, I've already experienced significant improvements in energy, mood, and focus, and my lichen sclerosus is about 99% better.

I switched from the steroid cream my gynecologist prescribed for the lichen sclerosis— which suppresses the immune system. Instead, I began using a customized cream from my compounding pharmacy designed to support and rebalance it. The difference is amazing. Unlike traditional pharmacies, compounding pharmacies create personalized medications by adjusting dosages, removing allergens, or offering more natural alternatives to meet individual needs.

I'm also avoiding alcohol and long, hot baths, as heat and moisture can exacerbate my condition—even with filtered water. With these changes, I'm confident my health will continue to improve, and I finally feel in control again. Praise God!

No matter where you are in your health journey, small, mindful steps can help you take control of your toxic load to improve your overall well-being.

Remember, detoxification isn't just about physical toxins. It encompasses:

- **Mental well-being:** Addressing negative thought patterns.
- **Emotional health:** Processing suppressed emotions.
- **Spiritual wellness:** Resolving guilt, finding purpose.
- **Relationships:** Setting boundaries with toxic people.

True detoxification is a holistic process that involves continually cleansing the body, mind, and spirit for lasting well-being. It's not about drastic cleanses, but consistent, mindful choices.

The body is designed to be self-healing. Often, our role is simply to clear obstacles and create an environment conducive to healing.

Consider this: If a fish gets sick, do you treat the fish or clean up the environment that made the fish sick?

CHAPTER 13

Empowered Parenting: Shaping Healthy Futures

Lo, children are an heritage of the Lord,
And the fruit of the womb is his reward.

(Psalm 127:3 *KJV*)

About ten years ago, I attended a chiropractic conference in California with my daughter and son-in-law. On the drive back to our hotel, the conversation turned to one of the presentations about food additives. My granddaughters, sitting in the backseat, listened intently as we explained how many of these additives found in everyday snacks, like fruit gummies, contained chemicals linked to cancer. Their young faces grew serious as they processed this unsettling information.

When they returned home, my daughter noticed something unusual. A full box of fruit snacks was in the trash. She called out, "Why are the fruit snacks in the trash?" Her five-year-old stepped forward and said, "I threw them out because I don't want cancer."

Years later, a similar moment unfolded with her cousin. After Halloween, he held out a handful of brightly wrapped candies and asked his mom, "Which of these have fake colors?" When she pointed to one of the packages, his face tightened with resolve, and he marched off with it. His mom asked, "Where are you going?" He turned back and replied, "To throw it in the trash."

These were proud moments for me as Yia Yia (Greek for grandmother). You may wonder what made my grandchildren willingly part with these treats.

A Generation in Peril, a Future at Stake

When we know better, we must do better—and it starts with the health and well-being of our children. The vitality of society, the strength of our economy, and the preservation of family values hinge on the well-being of the next generation. Yet, today's children are sicker than ever, and infertility rates have never been higher.

Chronic conditions and concerning health trends are now affecting millions of children, threatening not only their immediate health but also their long-term quality of life. The following statistics highlight the scope of this growing crisis:

- **Mental Health:** In 2023, CDC data revealed that 20% of U.S. high school students seriously considered attempting suicide in the past year, while 14% of adolescents take prescription medications for emotions, concentration, behavior, or mental health issues.

- **Diabetes:** Type 1 diabetes, one of the most common autoimmune diseases among children, has been steadily increasing. Type 2 diabetes, a lifestyle-related disease, doubled in youth aged 10 to 19 between 2002 and 2018. A study predicts that, if current trends continue, cases of type 1 diabetes in youth could rise by 65% by 2060, while type 2 diabetes could surge by nearly 700%. These figures do not account for undiagnosed cases or prediabetes, which may further compound the crisis.

- **Obesity:** Obesity rates among children and adolescents have tripled since the 1970s.
- **Fertility Rates:** U.S. fertility rates have been in decline for decades, reaching historic lows in both 2020 and 2023. Globally, infertility affects 20 to 30% of women in reproductive age, while approximately 15% of men experience infertility, with sperm counts halving over the past 40 years.
- **Heart Health:** In youth and professional sports—once a symbol of health—sudden cardiac events and myocarditis are becoming distressingly familiar headlines.
- **Military Eligibility:** The Pentagon reports that 77% of young Americans aged 17 to 24 are unfit for military service due to obesity, lack of education, drug use, and mental or physical health issues.

These trends don't represent the path God designed for us. They're the consequence of a world that has strayed from His wisdom. These conditions don't simply end in childhood; they ripple into adulthood, shaping physical health, mental resilience, and life opportunities. They threaten the stability of our society and the future of generations to come. A society that fails its children ultimately weakens its future.

However, this is not the end of the story. Scripture reminds us,

> *All your children shall be taught by the Lord,*
> *and great shall be the peace of your children.*

(Isaiah 54:13 *NKJV*)

Still, as Robert F. Kennedy, Jr. aptly observed, "There's nothing more profitable than a sick child."

What Are Parents to Do?

My mother always said, "Parenting is the toughest job with the least training and the most reward." She was right, and it's not getting easier. We live in an age where family dinners are replaced by solitary screen time, where the blue light of devices drowns out the warm glow of intergenerational connection. Kids are spending less time outdoors connecting to nature.

Processed foods and environmental toxins invade our homes, threatening our children's health, while technology disconnects us from each other and God. The enemy has crept into our lives, attacking the family's foundation and sowing seeds of distraction and disconnection.

Parenting today takes courage, intentionality, and a commitment to stand against unhealthy norms. It means raising children to embrace a better way—one built on health, wisdom, and resilience. Counter-cultural choices can be hard, but they open the door to real change, equipping our children to thrive in every area of life.

From preconception to the countless decisions of daily life, parents hold the incredible power to shape their children's futures. It all begins with being informed and intentional.

Do not conform to the pattern of this world,
but be transformed by the renewing of your mind.

(Romans 12:2 *NIV*)

Preconception to Pregnancy

The journey to parenthood begins even before conception. Lifestyle choices like diet and exercise, as well as toxin exposure significantly impact sperm and egg quality. For men, habits such as smoking, drinking, and poor diet can lower sperm count and reduce motility.

Women's egg quality is also affected by these behaviors, leading to fertility problems or increased risks of birth defects.

After conception, the fetus's health depends heavily on the mother's environment and choices. What a mother eats during pregnancy and breastfeeding can influence her child's taste preferences. Flavors transfer to amniotic fluid and breast milk, shaping the baby's acceptance of foods later. Research also shows that umbilical cords contain an average of over 200 toxins, indicating significant exposure during pregnancy.

Sadly, pregnant women are often encouraged to make medical choices without being fully informed. For example, they may be told to get vaccines that haven't been tested with placebo-controlled studies or properly researched for pregnant women. This "womb-to-grave" approach to medical treatments begins before birth and continues throughout life.

Within the first day or two of life, before a newborn's immune system has developed, they are routinely subjected to:

- **Antibiotic eye ointment**
- **Vitamin K injection** containing polysorbate 80 (P80), propylene glycol, sodium acetate anhydrous, and glacial acetic acid. P80, commonly used in pharmaceuticals as a stabilizer and to enhance drug delivery to the brain, can disrupt the blood-brain barrier, allowing substances to pass through more easily.
- **Hepatitis B vaccine** containing aluminum, formaldehyde, yeast proteins, and in some formulations, P80. This vaccine protects against a disease transmitted through intravenous drug use or sexual contact—activities infants don't engage in. Mothers can be tested during pregnancy, more than once if necessary.
- **Circumcision**, which carries risks of bleeding, infection, injury to the penis, and possible breastfeeding difficulties, as well as long-term physical, sexual, and psychological impacts.

The choices parents make before birth and in their child's earliest days can shape their health for years to come.

Chiropractic for Healthy Beginnings

Chiropractic care can play a powerful role from pregnancy through childhood. Proper alignment during pregnancy can improve mobility, reduce pain, and even aid in childbirth. When my youngest grand-daughter was born, her head wasn't positioned properly in the birth canal to initiate the next phase of labor—she was stuck. My daughter (a chiropractor) asked her husband (also a chiropractor) to adjust her and guided him on exactly how to do it. The baby was born soon after.

Chiropractic adjustments for newborns can help ensure their spines are properly aligned and nerve communication is functioning well. Even gentle vaginal births can place strain on a baby's spine, and caesarean births can be even more traumatic. Removing interference in a new-born's nerve conduction supports healthy development from the start.

In my own family and others, I've observed that children who grow up with regular chiropractic care seem healthier, more resilient, and better able to handle life's challenges. These vibrant, active kids rarely need antibiotics or other medications.

As children grow, new challenges emerge—especially when it comes to making healthy choices in a world filled with harmful influences.

Outsmarting the Food Industry

Even as toddlers, children are bombarded with messages about un-healthy food choices. Food companies spend billions marketing junk food to kids because it works. They use bright packaging, superheroes, and catchy jingles to create emotional connections. It's hard for kids to resist these temptations when they're everywhere, often placed at their eye level in stores.

Food marketing strongly influences how kids view what's good, with potentially lasting effects on eating habits. While some children outgrow unhealthy eating, research shows most do not. These marketing efforts target children as if they make the purchasing decisions—because often, they do. The food industry thrives on a lack of awareness, so understanding their tactics makes it harder for them to manipulate our choices.

> *"The only thing more powerful*
> *than marketing is parenting."*
>
> —Dr. Sachin Patel

Parents need to recognize their power to counter these influences and guide children toward healthier choices. Studies show the family environment, whether beneficial or not, plays a pivotal role in shaping a child's eating behavior. Let's explore ways to outsmart the junk food industry and make healthy food appealing to kids.

Creating a Healthy Food Environment

Raising healthy eaters isn't just about serving good meals; it's about teaching kids how food affects their health and how they feel. When they understand this, they're more likely to make better choices and take ownership of what they eat.

While my granddaughter confidently tossed the fruit snacks years ago, her dietary journey hasn't been without detours. Like many teens, she explored less-than-ideal foods. Living in Hawaii, she experienced severe allergic responses to dairy but later reintroduced it. Recently, though, she's rediscovered the importance of listening to her body—realizing gluten isn't a good fit for her. This ability to self-correct stems from education and empowerment. Even when kids stray, planting seeds of awareness early helps them return to healthier choices.

Creating a positive food environment starts with the food you bring into your home and helping kids appreciate good eating habits and caring for their bodies. Kids also learn by watching, so your example is key. Sharing family meals creates positive experiences and meaningful routines, strengthening family bonds. Studies show children who regularly eat with their families tend to eat better, perform better in school, and are less likely to struggle with obesity—even as adults.

Train up a child in the way he should go, and when he is old, he will not depart from it.

(Proverbs 22:6 *KJV*)

Tips for Younger Kids

When it comes to younger children, your influence is especially strong. The following dos and don'ts can help establish a solid foundation for healthy eating habits.

Dos:

- **Make healthy eating fun:** Rename foods with superhero or silly names like "X-ray Vision Carrots" to spark imagination.
- **Get creative with plating:** Arrange colorful fruits and veggies into fun shapes. My grandchildren and I have made palm trees, caterpillars, flowers, and bears out of various fruits and vegetables.
- **Offer healthy snacks:** Keep cut-up fruits and vegetables easily accessible, even on the go, but don't let them snack close to mealtime.
- **Connect kids to food:** Teach them where food comes from through gardening, farm visits, or farmers' markets.

- **Encourage healthy peers:** Food marketers understand that kids want to be like their peers, so organize playdates with like-minded families to counter marketing influences.

- **Cook together:** Cooking is a valuable life skill, and kids take pride in eating what they help make. With practice, their skills will improve, making it a worthwhile time investment.

- **Utilize health apps:** Introduce kids to apps like Yuka, which scan food barcodes to provide health scores, explain nutritional quality, highlight harmful additives, and suggest healthier alternatives. Younger children may need help, but using the app together can make learning about food choices fun!

Don'ts:

- **Don't use strict bans:** Studies show forbidden foods often become more desirable as children grow up.

- **Don't tie food to emotions:** Avoid guilt, rewards, or affection tied to food, which can lead to long-term conditioning and unhealthy relationships with treats.

- **Don't focus only on health:** Convince kids that healthy food also tastes good.

- **Don't buy junk food:** Prolonging removal sends mixed signals.

- **Don't rush meals:** Encourage proper chewing and slow eating to aid digestion.

- **Don't make food a battleground:** Power struggles over food undermine its purpose as nourishment.

I confess to doing my share of Don'ts. For example, when my step-daughter was little, she was always the last one to finish eating. I regret rushing her because the rest of us were probably eating too fast. So, give yourself grace but stay committed. This early foundation lays the groundwork for helping kids develop a positive relationship with food.

Guiding Teens

As children grow older, your influence shifts. Teens often make food choices outside the home—at school, with friends, or with their own money. While you can't control every decision, you're still the parent in your home and likely make most purchasing decisions. Involve them in meal planning and cooking to give them a sense of ownership. When teens feel heard, they're more likely to listen.

For teens, like my granddaughter, who have strayed and are finding their way back, it's a reminder that empowerment and education work—even if it takes time. Keep planting seeds of awareness, because the foundation you've built gives them the tools to make better decisions over time.

Parenting isn't easy, but instilling healthy habits is invaluable. While it's tempting to give in to demands for junk food—especially when you're rushed or tired—consistency is key. Scripture reminds us of the importance of persistence:

> *These words that I am giving you today are to be in your heart. Repeat them to your children. Talk about them when you sit in your house and when you walk along the road, when you lie down and when you get up.*
>
> (Deuteronomy 6:6-7 CSB)

Even picky eaters can learn to appreciate new tastes with encouragement and repeated exposure. Kids are naturally fearful of new foods, so don't give up—and avoid projecting your own fears or dislikes onto them. Let them decide for themselves, but encourage them to try at least one bite every time a food is served. Studies show that it may take kids 8 to 12 exposures to accept a food. If they choose not to eat it, don't offer an alternate meal or snack shortly after the meal. Hunger will help them appreciate what's on the table next time.

Sometimes, a little creativity helps. For example, when my son was about two, he didn't like spinach the first time he tried it. The next time we had spinach, I told him, "It's just for adults." Naturally, he wanted some and decided he liked it. This approach shows how curiosity and reversed expectations can make a big difference.

While creative strategies like this can help with picky eating, raising healthy children involves much more than what's on their plates. For additional tips on taste-training to overcome picky eating, check out the Resources online.

Beyond the Plate

Building a strong spiritual foundation and limiting harmful exposures are equally important. Tackling modern challenges like screen time, exercise, and sleep is key to creating a balanced, healthy environment.

Limit Sedentary Habits

Encouraging kids to be active and limiting screen time is vital for their mental and physical health. Excessive screen use—more than one hour daily for children under age five or two hours for older ones—is linked to behavior issues, sleep problems, and difficulties with focus and memory. Chronic overstimulation during critical brain development can cause cognitive impairments resembling early dementia in adults. Studies suggest it may also accelerate brain aging, raising the risk of dementia later in life.

Physical activity reduces stress, improves focus, and counters these effects. Instead of screens, encourage outdoor play, creative hobbies, or family activities like hiking, biking, ping-pong, or basketball. Time in nature reduces stress, boosts mood, and strengthens family bonds. Simple activities like backyard games, park visits, or walking the dog nurture a love for the outdoors while supporting a healthy, active lifestyle.

Prioritize Sleep—Especially for Teens

Adequate sleep is vital for all children but especially for teens, who need 8 to 10 hours per night for growth and development. Yet many teens fall short due to late-night screen use, early school start times, and social pressures. Additionally, teens' biological clocks naturally shift, making it harder for them to fall asleep early.

Chronic sleep deprivation can lead to:

- Poor academic performance
- Increased mental health risks
- Impaired decision-making and risky behaviors
- Long-term physical health issues, like obesity and cardiovascular disease

To help your teen establish better sleep habits:

- **Educate and Empower:** Discuss the importance of sleep, how it affects their health, and good sleep habits as outlined in chapter 11.
- **Establish a Routine:** Create a consistent bedtime schedule that allows for 8 to 10 hours of sleep.
- **Limit Screen Time Before Bed:** Enforce a "screens off" policy at least one hour before bedtime. Most WiFi routers can be programmed to turn off internet access on a schedule for specific devices.
- **Create a Sleep-Friendly Environment:** Ensure their room is cool, dark, and quiet, with a comfortable mattress and pillow.

Support your teen by helping them balance homework and extracurricular activities and let them sleep in on weekends when possible. Building healthy sleep habits takes time, but the rewards are well worth it for their physical, mental, and emotional well-being.

Putting Empowered Parenting into Action:

Parenting isn't easy, but small, consistent changes create lasting impact. Raising healthy kids in today's world can feel daunting, but small, consistent changes can create lasting impact. While these steps may seem overwhelming at first, remember that you don't have to implement them all at once. The journey doesn't require perfection—just intentionality and persistence. You have the power to shape your children's health and future, starting with these simple, actionable steps:

1. **Prepare for Pregnancy and Research Carefully:** Parents should focus on improving their health, reducing their toxic load before conception, and making informed decisions during pregnancy. Use independent sources like PubMed, prioritizing peer-reviewed studies, and investigate ingredients in anything you put on or in your body. (See chapter 12 for tips on reducing toxins.)

2. **Create a Healthy Home Environment:** Make your home a place where healthy choices are easy and accessible. Stock nutritious, whole-food alternatives and eliminate the temptation of unhealthy options. Encourage family meals as a time to connect and share good food together.

3. **Educate and Empower:** Teach your children about health and nutrition in age-appropriate ways. Help them understand the "why" behind healthy choices by explaining food labels, nutrition basics, and how diet affects their bodies. Empower them to make informed decisions within clear boundaries, fostering lifelong habits.

4. **Prepare for Success:** Get the whole family involved in meal planning, grocery shopping, and food prep. Focus on simple, wholesome ingredients rather than expensive, processed "health" products. Engaging children in the process teaches them essential life skills and makes them more invested in healthy eating.

5. **Model Self-Care:** Parenting is demanding, but self-care isn't selfish—it's essential. The first step in raising healthy children is modeling health-promoting behavior. By prioritizing your own health, you're also better equipped to care for your children. Set clear screen-time boundaries for everyone and get sufficient sleep and physical activity. Even simple activities, like walking laps during your kids' sports practices, can make a difference.

By taking these steps, we can nurture a generation of children who are not only healthier but also empowered to make wise decisions about their well-being for a lifetime. These habits won't just shape their futures—they have the potential to influence future generations through epigenetics.

Empowering the Next Generation

So, what made my grandchildren willingly part with those treats?

It wasn't because they were forced or shamed into it. The truth is children are capable of making surprisingly mature decisions when given the right information in a way they can understand. We didn't just tell them to avoid artificial colors—we explained how these additives affect the body and let them decide. That choice—free from pressure—allowed them to take ownership of their health. And they did.

Changing habits in a world of convenience isn't easy. I get it. Packed schedules, rising food costs, family resistance, conflicting nutrition advice, and the demands of sports and social activities make it even harder. But following *God's Prescription* will help you navigate these challenges, and I promise—the rewards are worth it.

You are an amazing parent for taking charge of your child's health. Our children are the future, and it's time to reclaim their well-being. This means returning to timeless truths: nourishing their bodies with whole foods, their minds with wisdom, and their spirits with love and presence.

When we equip our children with knowledge and tools to make informed choices, we aren't just shaping their future—we're shaping future generations. Imagine the ripple effect of these choices in your family. How far could they reach?

This also means supporting healthy habits across generations. Grandparents, be mindful not to undermine what parents are building—loading kids up with sugar and sending them home only makes it harder. Instead, reinforce their foundation by offering nourishing treats and setting a lasting example.

As we move into the next chapter, take time to reflect on how these timeless principles apply throughout every stage of life.

> *I have no greater joy than to hear that*
> *my children walk in truth.*
>
> (3 John 1:4 *NKJV*)

CHAPTER 14

Numbering Our Days:
Living Fully and Dying Well

"It's not the years in your life that matter,
but the life in your years."

—Attributed to Abraham Lincoln

As a functional medicine student, I observed an elderly patient and was stunned to count twelve prescriptions. My supervisor shook her head and said, "That's nothing compared to some seniors."

Years later, those words proved prophetic with my own father. Dad was once incredibly active—playing and refereeing sports and running his tire dealership. Then, an ankle injury and retirement led to a sedentary lifestyle. His health spiraled downward: metabolic syndrome, diabetes, cancers, cardiac events, and pneumonia. Still, doctors marveled at his resilience.

But his body couldn't keep up forever. One day, he collapsed at home and was taken to the hospital. While there, I noticed a disturbing pattern: he felt well in the morning but worsened after taking his medications and stopped eating. After several requests, I obtained his medication list. It contained 24 items, including some that had previously caused reactions!

His doctor agreed it was excessive. After reducing his medications to only essentials, my dad began to rally. It was bittersweet; it became clear my parents could no longer care for each other. My mother had cognitive and balance issues, and my father's condition had worsened. We made the difficult decision to transition them to assisted living, believing it would be a safe, active, and social environment.

Then COVID hit. Instead of community and connection, my parents faced isolation and restrictions. My dad fell, broke a rib, and was hospitalized for observation. While there, he was prescribed Tramadol, which caused severe confusion. His hearing aid battery died, leaving him unable to hear his therapists, who labeled him uncooperative. He couldn't understand why we weren't with him. Calls were difficult due to his confusion. He was quickly going downhill.

After I lobbied for visitation rights, my dad rallied enough to go home. But once back in assisted living, isolation resumed and his spirit faded. Despite doctors' best intentions, the system failed him. While Dad's death certificate reads "congestive heart failure," I believe the emotional toll of COVID protocols ultimately ended his life.

As I watched my dad decline, I wondered: Was this what aging had to look like? Or was there another way?

On the other hand, there was Bud Smith, my high school best friend's father—a man I affectionately called "Dad," too. He taught me to water ski, and his family was always on the move—skiing, camping, and adventuring together. Bud stayed active throughout his life, running his electrical business and doing calisthenics every morning.

After retiring, Bud and his wife, Madonna, spent winters in Arizona, embracing an active senior community. During this time, Bud learned to swim and played tennis until the age of 94. He kept riding his bike until his balance made it unsafe. He faithfully performed his daily calisthenics until the week before his passing at 98.

The contrast between my father's story and Bud's couldn't be more striking. My dad's health steadily declined, burdened by chronic conditions and a mountain of medications, while Bud thrived, living fully until the very end.

What was Bud's secret? Was it staying active, his social connections, or a combination of choices? And how might understanding Bud's approach make a difference for the rest of us?

Mechanisms of Aging and How *God's Prescription* Addresses Them

Certain changes in the body are inevitable with aging, even with a healthy diet and lifestyle. Over time, wear and tear and gravity take their toll. As Atul Gawande wrote in *Being Mortal*, "But the decline does march on, as inexorable as fall following summer." Scripture confirms his observation:

> *For even though our outer person gradually wears out, our*
> *inner being is renewed every single day.*

(2 Corinthians 4:16 *TPT*)

While aging cannot be stopped, its speed and severity are not fixed. Modern lifestyles—marked by stress, poor diets, and inactivity—often accelerate decline. In contrast, the habits outlined in *God's Prescription* can slow or even counteract many of these processes.

The following key mechanisms of aging reveal how *God's Prescription* supports aging gracefully and living fully:

1. **Telomere Shortening:** Telomeres—the protective caps on our chromosomes—shorten with age, leading to cell damage.

God's Prescription:

- The AIRD's polyphenols and antioxidants (berries, leafy greens, cruciferous vegetables) protect telomeres and support repair.
- Prayer, mindfulness, and deep breathing help reduce oxidative stress, a key driver of telomere shortening.
- Regular physical activity further reduces oxidative stress and inflammation, promoting telomere health.

2. **Mitochondrial Dysfunction:** Mitochondria—the cells' energy producers—decline in efficiency and number, reducing energy and increasing oxidative stress.

God's Prescription:

- Resistance training stimulates the creation of new mitochondria and improves efficiency.
- Nutrient-dense foods (leafy greens, berries, and healthy fats with CoQ10, B vitamins, and antioxidants) enhance mitochondrial function.
- Intermittent fasting boosts mitochondrial efficiency and promotes autophagy to clear out damaged mitochondria.
- Stress management practices (see chapter 11) reduce oxidative damage.

3. **Senescent (Zombie) Cells:** Senescent cells stop dividing but remain in the body, driving inflammation and impairing tissue repair.

God's Prescription:

- Antioxidant-rich foods (berries, leafy greens, cruciferous vegetables) reduce oxidative stress and cellular damage.
- Exercise and intermittent fasting stimulate autophagy to clear damaged cells.
- Stress reduction lowers cellular stress and inflammation.

4. **DNA Damage:** DNA accumulates damage from free radicals, toxins, and metabolic stress, disrupting cellular communication and function.

God's Prescription:

- Antioxidants and polyphenols (berries, green tea, and dark leafy greens) protect DNA from oxidative stress.
- Cruciferous vegetables, omega-3-rich foods (fatty fish, walnuts), folate (legumes, avocados), and zinc (grass-fed beef, pumpkin seeds) support DNA repair.
- Stress reduction reduces DNA damage and enhances cellular repair.

5. **Stem Cell Exhaustion:** Stem cells, which repair and regenerate tissues, decline in both numbers and efficiency.

God's Prescription:

- The AIRD provides essential vitamins and minerals for stem cell health.
- Resistance and weight-bearing exercise stimulate stem cell activity.
- Adequate sleep and stress reduction promote stem cell function.

6. **Loss of Muscle Mass and Bone Density:** Sarcopenia and bone mineral loss increase the risk of weakness, fractures, and falls.

God's Prescription:

- Strength training and weight-bearing exercises maintain muscle and bone strength.
- Protein-rich foods (grass-fed meat, legumes, nuts) support muscle repair and growth.
- Calcium and vitamin D (leafy greens, supplements) promote bone density.

7. **Gut Health and Inflammaging:** Imbalances in gut bacteria contribute to leaky gut and chronic inflammation (inflammaging).

   God's Prescription:

   - The AIRD's fiber-rich foods (vegetables, fruits, gluten-free grains) nourish beneficial gut bacteria.
   - Fermented foods (sauerkraut, kefir) provide probiotics for microbiome health.
   - Anti-inflammatory spices (turmeric, ginger) help reduce inflammation.
   - Exercise and stress management improve gut health and lower inflammation.

God's Prescription supports healthy aging beyond these mechanisms. Anti-inflammatory foods like sweet potatoes, bananas, and spinach promote cardiovascular health, while regular exercise strengthens the heart and enhances circulation.

Lifelong learning, social interactions, and spiritual practices like meditation and prayer sharpen the mind and reduce stress. Consuming antioxidant-rich, omega-3 foods like fatty fish, walnuts, and chia seeds helps combat brain inflammation. Hydration and nutrient-dense foods, including citrus fruits, bell peppers, and bone broth, support collagen production and skin elasticity.

While aging increases chronic disease risk, these conditions are not inevitable. Aging isn't just determined by years lived—it's influenced by factors like oxidative stress, chronic inflammation, and cellular damage. These mechanisms don't just contribute to aging; they create conditions for chronic disease to develop.

Biological age measures how well your body functions and can differ from chronological age. By making strategic lifestyle changes, you can slow biological aging, lower disease risk, and even feel younger. (Curious about your biological age? Take the quiz in the Resources!)

As demonstrated in my father's and Bud's stories, maintaining physical health is key to aging well. Strength, balance, flexibility, and cardiovascular fitness are essential for staying independent and living fully. Let's explore how to maintain or regain these vital aspects.

Maintaining Mobility and Independence

*"Nobody can go back and start a new beginning,
but anyone can start today and make a new ending."*

—Maria Robinson, American writer

As Christians, we may not fear death, but losing independence is a common concern. The loss of muscle strength, flexibility, and balance increases the risk of falls and the need for assistance.

After age 30, muscle mass typically decreases by 3 to 8% per decade, totaling up to a 24% loss by age 60. After 60, the rate of loss accelerates. Muscle strength declines even faster, especially after 75, with yearly losses of 3 to 4% for men and 2.5 to 3% for women. Inactivity significantly worsens this decline.

If you have constipation, tight muscles, stiff joints, shortness of breath, or low mood, your body may need more movement. Regular activity promotes bowel regularity, muscle flexibility, joint lubrication, improved heart and lung capacity, and boosts happy hormones.

The good news is that our bodies can transform at any age. A study of nursing home residents around 90 years old revealed that strength training nearly tripled their muscle strength, increased thigh muscle size by 9%, and improved walking speed by 48%! It's never too late to start.

While walking and enjoyable activities are excellent ways to begin, incorporating other exercises can further enhance health and longevity. Always consult your healthcare provider before starting a new fitness program, especially if you have pre-existing health conditions.

Exercise for Every Stage of Life

The following physical activity guidelines are based on evidence-based recommendations for optimal health and longevity:

- **Preschoolers (ages 3 to 5)** should be active throughout the day to foster growth and development.

- **Children and Adolescents (ages 6 to 17)** should engage in at least 60 minutes of moderate-to-vigorous activity daily, including vigorous intensity and muscle-strengthening exercises at least three times a week.

- **Adults (ages 18 to 64)** should aim for 150 to 300 minutes of moderate-intensity aerobic activity or 75 to 150 minutes of vigorous activity weekly. Additional benefits occur beyond 300 minutes.

- **Older Adults** should follow the adult guidelines while adjusting intensity to personal fitness levels and chronic conditions. If unable to meet these guidelines, remain as physically active as your abilities allow.

Strength Training

Strength training is critical for maintaining muscle mass and function:

- **Children and Adolescents (ages 6 to 17):** Engage in muscle-strengthening exercises at least three days a week.

- **Adults:** Train each major muscle group on two or more days a week. This can be done in one session or spread across multiple days.
  - Adults under 65 should perform exercises to fatigue or until they can no longer maintain proper form.
  - Adults over 65 should aim for moderate to high intensity, around 50 to 70% of maximum effort.

Key muscle groups to include in your routine:

- **Lower Body:** Calves, quadriceps (front thighs), hamstrings (back thighs), and glutes.
- **Upper Body:** Shoulders, chest, upper back, biceps, and triceps.
- **Core:** Abdominals, lower back, and obliques (side muscles).

Even small areas like hands, feet, and the neck benefit from regular movement. Isometric exercises, which involve holding a position, can easily be done while watching TV. Going barefoot, when safe, helps strengthen the feet, improving coordination and balance.

Always warm up before exercise and stretch after each workout. Don't overdo it, especially if you haven't worked out in a while! Start light and gradually increase intensity to avoid injury.

Balance Training to Prevent Falls

Balance declines with age, increasing the risk of falls and injuries. To improve stability and maintain independence, incorporate balance exercises at least three times a week:

- **Single-Leg Stands:** Stand on one leg for 10 to 30 seconds, then switch.
- **Heel-to-Toe Walk:** Walk in a straight line, positioning the heel of one foot directly in front of the toes of the other. Perform near a sturdy surface for support if needed.
- **Chair Stands:** Sit and stand without using your hands to build lower-body strength.
- **Tai Chi or Qi Gong:** Proven to enhance balance and coordination.

Tips: Strengthen leg and core muscles, wear supportive shoes, and remove tripping hazards. Small efforts can significantly reduce fall risk and keep you moving confidently.

You don't need a gym membership or expensive equipment to get started. Resistance bands, ankle weights, and dumbbells are affordable and effective tools. However, gyms offer personal trainers and introductory sessions helpful for beginners. Fitness professionals can ensure safe form to prevent injury. If you prefer home workouts, many trainers and physical therapists share excellent free content on YouTube.

Establish your "why" for getting fit—whether it's staying independent, playing with your grandkids, or simply feeling stronger. Set realistic goals, take the first step, and remember: It's never too late to start.

Nutritional Support for Aging

Exercise stimulates muscle growth, but proper nutrition provides the necessary building blocks. While the AIRD guidelines are anti-aging, the aging body sometimes needs extra support. Building anything, including muscle, requires the right materials.

The following nutrients and strategies can help support your body as it ages:

1. **Quality Protein:** Older adults need moderately higher protein intake to combat muscle loss and build muscle. Below are the current recommendations:

   - **For combating muscle loss:** 0.45 to 0.68 grams per pound of body weight daily (77 to 116 grams for a 170-pound person and 90 to 136 grams for a 200-pound person).

   - **For building muscle:** 0.8 to 1.0 grams per pound of body weight daily (136 to 170 grams for a 170-pound person and 160 to 200 grams for a 200-pound person).

To put these amounts into perspective, a large chicken breast has about 26 grams, a quarter-pound of grass-fed ground beef 20 to 25 grams, and an egg 6 grams.

2. **Whey Protein Isolate:** This powdered form of protein from dairy is quickly digested and absorbed, making it ideal for post-workout recovery or pre-workout smoothies. It's particularly helpful for individuals with reduced appetites or those struggling to meet protein needs through whole foods. Because the whey is isolated from casein, it's often better tolerated than other dairy products. For non-dairy alternatives, consider pea or hemp protein.

3. **Carbohydrates:** Carbs help repair microscopic muscle tears incurred during exercise and fuel the muscle-building process. For pre-workout nutrition, easily digestible carbs from fruits are preferable. Focus on complex carbohydrates like quinoa or sweet potatoes for sustained energy. Avoid refined sugars or sports drinks.

4. **Protein and Carbohydrate Combo:** Consuming protein with carbohydrates before or after resistance training can optimize muscle repair and growth. For example, try a smoothie with protein powder and a banana or berries.

5. **Creatine Monohydrate:** Research shows that creatine supplementation, when combined with resistance training, helps older adults maintain muscle strength and mass. While creatine is synthesized in the body from amino acids, it is also found in seafood and red meat. Supplements provide a convenient way to increase intake. Taking creatine post-workout can help replenish energy and support recovery.

6. **Collagen:** Collagen supports skin elasticity, joint health, and the body's structure. Collagen production decreases with age, so supplementation can help maintain skin hydration, reduce wrinkles, and support bone and joint health. Collagen powder can be added to beverages, soups, or baked goods for an easy boost that doesn't affect taste.

Individual needs may vary based on age, activity level, and overall health. Consult a nutrition professional for personal guidance on dosing and suitability.

The Gifts of Aging: Embracing Life's Later Seasons

Wisdom is found with the elderly,
and understanding comes with long life.

(Job 12:12 *CSB*)

While society often fixates on avoiding aging, chasing the elusive fountain of youth through medical advancements and anti-aging products, there is wisdom in embracing the natural process of growing older. Following *God's Prescription* can enhance our quality of life and perhaps reduce the need for medical interventions.

Aging is a blessing not granted to all. With it comes hard-earned wisdom, greater self-confidence, and freedom from many societal pressures. Scripture reminds us that later years can be among our most fruitful:

Even in old age they will still produce fruit;
they will remain vital and green.

(Psalm 92:14 *NLT*)

Retirement, from a biblical view, isn't about stopping but entering a new season of purpose. It's an opportunity to pursue delayed projects, learn new skills, or embark on overdue adventures—free from career pressures. This transition invites us to realign our priorities and focus on what truly matters from an eternal perspective.

Aging also challenges us to let go—of possessions, roles, and even certain abilities. While this can be difficult, it creates space for growth, deeper spiritual connection, and a renewed focus on leaving a meaningful legacy.

Death, like aging, is part of God's design—an earthly end and the beginning of eternity. Living fully means making the most of the time we're given, while dying well means preparing spiritually, emotionally, and practically. Both require intentional choices aligned with our faith and values.

Action Steps for Living Fully and Dying Well

Here are some key steps to help you navigate this season with purpose and peace:

1. **Avoid the "prescribing cascade."** A prescribing cascade occurs when side effects from one medication are misinterpreted as new medical conditions, leading to additional prescriptions. Collaborate with a functional medicine practitioner to identify and address the root causes of health issues, ensuring each medication's necessity. Regularly review your prescriptions to avoid situations like my father's, where numerous medications made it challenging to determine the cause of side effects.

2. **Advocate for yourself in healthcare settings.** Ensure you or a trusted person can make informed medical decisions. During COVID, my dad's experience without family advocacy highlighted the importance of having someone to speak on your behalf. Many patients faced similar challenges during COVID and some died without seeing their loved ones.

3. **Plan for the future.** Establish your will, power of attorney, and advance healthcare directives now to ensure your wishes are clear before a crisis arises.

4. **Find purpose and meaning in your later years.** Engage in mentoring, volunteering, deepening relationships, or serving your community or church. Seek God's guidance to continue bearing fruit in this season.

5. **Have uncomfortable conversations.** Clearly document and communicate your preferences regarding resuscitation, palliative care, and hospice to your loved ones while you're able.

6. **Ask questions and mend relationships.** Don't delay asking a loved one about things you've always wanted to know. Pursue reconciliation in strained relationships while there's still time.

Teach us to number our days,
that we may gain a heart of wisdom.

(Psalm 90:12 *NIV*)

A Tale of Two Aging Journeys

My father's and Bud's contrasting paths through their later years offer valuable lessons on aging. Dad, despite his resilience, faced numerous health challenges exacerbated by inactivity and overmedication, dying in hospice care. His struggle underscores the importance of proactive health management. Bud, staying active until the week before he died, exemplified vibrant aging through physical activity, strong relationships, and purposeful living.

These men's stories illustrate how our choices profoundly impact aging. While genetics contribute about 10% to longevity, the remaining 90% is shaped by lifestyle choices that influence gene expression. Their experiences remind us that the habits we cultivate shape not just our present, but our future well-being and quality of life.

I will be the same until your old age, and I will bear you up
when you turn gray. I have made you, and I will carry you; I
will bear and rescue you.

(Isaiah 46:4 *CSB*)

Faith, Reconciliation, and Living Fully

With the stories of my dad and Bud in mind, I am reminded that aging well is about far more than just physical health. It's about cultivating faith, reconciling relationships, and embracing each day as a gift.

My dear friend, Debbie Hurley, a retired hospice nurse, has shared profound insights from her years caring for the dying. In all her experience, she encountered only two patients who were truly bitter or angry. Everyone else, even in pain, understood that every day was a gift.

She also witnessed how deeply relationships matter at the end of life. Patients often hold on, waiting for reconciliation with an estranged loved one. One patient longed for her daughter, Laurie, to come, but Laurie never did. In desperation, she began calling Debbie "Laurie." In those final moments, Debbie became Laurie for her, offering the peace of connection she had been waiting for.

What struck Debbie most was the stark difference between those with faith and those without it. Many patients, as they neared the end, described seeing loved ones who had passed or experiencing moments of profound clarity.

But for those without faith, the experience was entirely different. Debbie recalled the terror in their eyes as they stared into the corners of the room, as if seeing something unimaginable. She had no idea what they were seeing. However, the contrast was undeniable. Those who knew Jesus died in peace, while those who didn't seemed gripped by fear.

These stories remind us of what truly matters. Do you want your loved ones to face death in terror, seeing what lies ahead without the hope of salvation? Or do you want them to die in peace, knowing they'll soon be with their Savior? If you haven't shared Jesus with those closest to you, don't wait—tomorrow isn't promised.

Final Thoughts

Reclaiming your God-given health begins now. Throughout *God's Prescription*, we've explored how deeply interconnected our health is with our daily choices. God designed our bodies to thrive when we align with His perfect design—nourishing ourselves with whole foods, embracing rest, and living with purpose. Yet, the world constantly tempts us with quick fixes, processed foods, and distractions that pull us away from His provision. Following *God's Prescription* isn't just helpful—it's essential.

Food is more than sustenance—it is sacred. Throughout Scripture, God used food to teach deeper truths, yet modern farming and food processing have stripped much of His creation of its purity. Food is part of our worship, our fellowship, and our healing. It evokes memories, fosters community, and unites cultures. To truly nourish ourselves, we must return to clean, unaltered foods, such as wild-caught fish, pasture-raised lamb, natural sea salt, and fermented olives. The closer we stick to His original design, the greater the blessing.

Our lives, too, have been shaped by a culture that prioritizes convenience over connection, busyness over balance, indulgence over intention. But God invites us to slow down—to truly savor the richness of life.

People say, "You must love to cook." I say, "No, I love to eat." And God delights in that. He gave us taste buds—not just to warn us of spoiled food, but to enjoy the goodness of His creation. We can savor food and life when we align with His ways—experiencing joy, connection, and deep fulfillment.

It's time to stop making excuses or blaming others or circumstances. When Adam and Eve sinned, they immediately tried to shift the blame—Adam blamed Eve, and Eve blamed the serpent—but God called them to take responsibility (Genesis 3:12-13). Likewise, in Jesus' parable, the servant who buried his talent justified his inaction with excuses, blaming fear instead of stepping out in faith (Matthew 25:24-30).

But here's the good news: God isn't here to condemn you—He's here to equip you. He has already given you everything you need to walk in health. His grace is abundant and He is with you every step of the way.

Imagine waking up with renewed energy, moving through your day with clarity, purpose, and a deep connection to God. This isn't just a dream—it's what happens when you fully embrace *God's Prescription*.

God is calling you to reclaim your health and embrace the abundant life He designed. The choice is yours, and the time is now. Will you say yes?

> *Open your mouth and taste, open your eyes and see—*
> *how good God is. Blessed are you who run to him.*

(Psalm 34:8 *MSG*)

An Invitation to Eternal Life

Throughout this book, we've explored how to steward your body, renew your mind, and live fully in the time God has given you. But true wellness begins deeper—in the heart—with a relationship with Jesus Christ.

He is not just the Great Physician who heals our bodies—He is the Savior who heals our hearts and offers us eternal life. No diet, lifestyle, or supplement can provide the peace and assurance that comes from knowing your sins are forgiven and your eternity is secure.

If you've never fully surrendered your life to Jesus—or if you're unsure where you stand with Him—you can begin right now with a simple prayer of faith like this:

"Jesus, I recognize that I am a sinner in need of Your forgiveness. I believe You died on the cross for my sins and rose again so I could have eternal life. I leave behind my old ways and ask You to lead me into new life with You. Please come into my heart and be my Savior and Lord. Thank You for your unending love and for making me new. Amen."

Salvation doesn't require fancy words or religious rituals—just a willing heart and a desire to know and receive Him. If you prayed this prayer with sincerity, you are now part of God's family. Heaven rejoices, and so do I.

I encourage you to:

- Share your decision with someone who will encourage you.
- Read the Gospel of John in the New Testament to learn more about Jesus.
- Find a Bible-teaching church where you can grow in your faith.

Your journey toward health and eternity has just begun. May your life reflect God's goodness from this day forward.

References and Resources

Please see the References and Resources for each chapter at
https://TerriWard.com/Gods-Prescription-References/

Scripture Index

General Index

Acknowledgements

First, I'd like to thank my husband, Kerry Benedict, for supporting me through this and all my other endeavors, for being my sounding board, faithful first-round editor, and unwavering encourager. Thank you for never giving up on me.

A heartfelt thank you to my team at Best Seller Publishing for their hard work and support—especially Dagny Darnell and Matt Schnarr—for their invaluable guidance. You helped me embrace my authentic voice and trust that my unique perspective is exactly what God intended for this book.

I am deeply grateful to my editor, Tawni Kenworthy-Heinige, for using her gifts to fine-tune my manuscript with such care and diligence.

Thank you to my beta readers at Life Church. Your contributions and feedback helped refine this work and are greatly appreciated.

To my father—whose suffering provided both lessons and purpose—thank you for your love and support. I will see you again, in eternal terms, in the blink of an eye.

Thank you to Dr. Alex Vasquez for creating the master's program at the University of Western States, which forever changed my perspective on true health. Your generosity in sharing knowledge—and your encouragement to edit—helped me become a better writer.

A special thank you to my foreword authors, Mario Murillo and Dr. John Bartemus, for lending your voices and credibility to this project. Your words honored the heart of this message and set the tone I pray will reach those who need it most.

I am also grateful to the many individuals who graciously endorsed this book. Your confidence in *God's Prescription* and your public encouragement mean more to me than words can express.

Finally, to my friends and family who supported and encouraged me through this venture—thank you. I love you all.

About the Author

Terri Ward, MS, FNPT, CGP, is a functional nutritionist, author, and speaker dedicated to helping people claim their God-given health. After transforming her own health through nutrition and lifestyle changes, she left a successful career as a CPA to earn a Master of Science in Human Nutrition and Functional Medicine and two nutrition certifications.

Terri writes health articles rooted in peer-reviewed research and is the author of *Alkaline Diet Meal Prep* and *The Healing Diverticulitis Cookbook*. In *God's Prescription*, she connects Scripture and science to provide a clear path to true wellness. She is also the founder of Spice Cure, a company offering allergy-friendly spice blends made with clean, organic ingredients—the cure for boring food.

Terri and her husband have seven grandchildren. She enjoys gardening and creating delicious, nutritious recipes.

www.ingramcontent.com/pod-product-compliance
Lightning Source LLC
Chambersburg PA
CBHW051302120626
46547CB00015B/2051